THE UNHAPPY HEADTEACHER

NAVIGATING HEADSHIP AND FINDING JOY IN THE ROLE

NADIA HEWSTONE

authors
AND CO.

CONTENTS

Foreword   7

Introduction   9

1. DREAM BIG   15
Your Values   16
Your why   21
Your dreams   23

2. POWER PLANNING   27
Planning Steps   31
Meetings   35
Termly strategic checkpoint   41
Termly strategic meeting agenda   42
Monthly strategy meeting   44
Monthly strategic meeting agenda   44

3. HIGH TARIFF RELATIONSHIPS   46
Managing up   46
Working with external partners   51
School Governors   54
Find your tribe   55

4. THE PUPILS   62
Radical advocacy   64
Sweat the small stuff   66
Be non-judgmental   68
Fight their corner   71
When service to pupils goes wrong and
parents complain   77

5. LEADING TEACHERS   82

6. HORIZON SCANNING   99
   Litany Against Fear   99
   Education Endowment Fund (EEF)   102
   Charter College of Teaching   103
   Early Intervention Foundation (EIF)   103

7. BURNOUT   110
   If You Hit Burnout   111

8. BOREDOM   119
   If You Get Bored   119

9. BE ASSERTIVE   131
   Aggressive responses   132
   Passive responses   133
   The benefits of being assertive   135
   How to be assertive   137

10. FINAL WORDS   144
    What's next?   149

   Acknowledgements   155
   Bibliography   157

DEDICATION

For my Mum, who taught me that almost everything in life is negotiable.

I was in school before light because Sarah, my college tutor, was observing me teach. Like an elf in the night, I pattered down the corridor to the cupboard I shared with Amira and Michelle. It was Ramadan and Amira was fasting. Michelle on the other hand was fast developing an overeating stress response to lesson planning.

Ten minutes before Spanish with 8b, I strode back down the corridor, swept down the stairs, and greeted Sarah confidently. She had been talking to the deputy headteacher at the bottom of the stairs.

As I approached, he turned unexpectedly to me and said, 'Nadia, one day you'll be a headteacher.'

INTRODUCTION

Do you find yourself spinning in circles, unsure which challenge to tackle first? You are not alone. Many head-teachers attempt the impossible every day, arriving at school before sunrise, leaving after sunset, and not managing to complete a single task on their to-do list. Some heads find themselves involved in the most unlikely activities and rarely achieve what they set out to. They are left tired, irritable, unfulfilled, anxious, and often dehydrated and underfed. Some go home and drink wine; others binge eat; few sleep well. On top of that throw funding challenges, high stakes and high accountability pressures and many struggle to enjoy their work.

How can you possibly do things differently? The answer lies in strategy and mindset, which are underpinned by a clear set of values. With a few practical tools, deep self-belief and some knowledge-building, all headteachers can find their way to enjoying their role and feeling in control. I will show you some ways you can do this in this book.

I am Nadia, a certified executive school leadership coach and former headteacher. I qualified as a coach while still in headship as I wanted to become the best person I could be so I could lead more effectively. My team and I benefitted no end from my coaching knowledge. When I was ready to leave headship I founded Destino Coaching to help other headteachers.

I hit a wall three years into my headship. I had injured my spine and had become obsessed with work. Then a brutal Ofsted inspection devastated me. After a week of shuffling around, I found a way through the fog with the support of some great people. I spent all my savings on spinal surgery and gave up alcohol. I committed to some serious self-care and set about my work to be ready the next time Ofsted came knocking.

While others thought it was Ofsted that broke me, I was actually burned out from twenty-plus years of neglecting my own needs. I've since used everything I learned from this to support hundreds of headteachers.

The two years after inspection were exciting for me and my team and we built a great school. Then I got bored. It turns out I wasn't alone in this. Boredom is a common issue in headship. In this book, I'll explain why, as well as how to avoid it.

When you let go of your fears, commit to your truth and hold yourself to being strategic, you can have more impact, work shorter days and find time for food and water.

We need to hold on to our headteachers. Understanding the key challenges facing the profession and developing strategies to support you is essential if we want to keep schools running.

I have written this book for headteachers but it will also be useful to deputy headteachers. This book is for you if you want to tackle the problems that lead to personal and professional defeat. It will give you practical tools as well as a challenge to your thinking. If you feel unhappy in headship, I hope this book goes some way to helping you find fulfilment.

I was a school leader including a headteacher for twenty-two years and have coached over two hundred headteachers since setting up Destino Coaching. I am on a mission to empower headteachers as I believe you have the power to unlock positive potential in our society.

Through my experience, I have identified the two most common reasons people leave headship – burnout and boredom. In this book, I share strategies to help you prevent both and to find joy in the role.

Headteachers are operating within a broken system, brought about by year-on-year income reduction in funding. This is compounded by rising pressures to compensate for other public services, which are also in crisis. These facts now need to be considered in all aspects of decision-making in schools. This does not mean you need to be sad, downtrodden or beaten but you do need to be pragmatic. For example, many of my clients talk about no longer being able to deliver the quality of support that is needed for pupils with Special Education Needs and Disabilities (SEND). However, most recognise they *are* able to ensure their Special Education Needs Coordinator (SENCo) is as supported and effective as possible and that their teachers have strong knowledge of SEND.

Never have the Nolan Principles been more important in headship. Despite so many ministers in public office appearing to have little or no regard for these principles, they have a forever place in school leadership. High accountability measures could tempt headteachers to push the boundaries of integrity, without a standard that we hold public officers to, and education could lose its way. This would lead to poor outcomes for children and society as a whole. Throughout the book, I will remind you that strategy is meaningless without values and principles to underpin it.

Headteachers have the power to influence culture beyond their schools. We have to keep building school cultures that serve young people, which in turn influence the communities around them. We foster this key concept through the mentorship and coaching of new headteachers and deputy headteachers.

You can carry on 'fighting the good fight' and influencing how Multi Academy Trusts (MATs) and Local Authorities evolve in the next few years. I want to guide you in the ways you have influence, even when it feels you have none.

Emme Mitchell came to me, thinking her time as a headteacher may be up. She was stressed, tearful, angry and didn't know what more she could give her school community. We worked out what she wanted, which was to be successful in her role. We defined what she meant by success and worked together for a year to implement things that would help her get to her own success. In that time, she established a new senior team, started going to orchestra again, brought the magic of music to her school and saw pupil outcomes soar. I asked what had made the difference, and she said it was giving herself permission to lead her own way – she found her mojo again and is now thriving in headship.

This book will provide you with prompts to consider the values and principles that will define your strategy for your school. The tips and tools have been put together to support real headteachers who, like you, are determined to serve while the system stabilises. You may also reach a space from which you can see your role in how things unfold for the future of education. You are precious to your community and to society as a whole and I have written this book because I want you to flourish, even in this difficult context.

1

DREAM BIG

YOUR VALUES

You cannot set goals or plan your approach in headship until you are clear about your personal values. You were drawn to your school (or stayed there) because of your beliefs about the change that needs to be brought about in the world. Start here, and spend time thinking about it, not least because there will be many things thrown at you and you need a way of navigating what you embrace, what you reject and how you engage. Values give meaning to the plan you put in place to achieve your goals for your school.

While it is important to explore shared values with your community, this process starts with you and what matters to you, the leader of the school. I will share some helpful journalling prompts with you later in the chapter. Journalling has many benefits: in this context, it helps you commit your beliefs to writing. Writing down your values and how they came to shape you, helps you develop your sense of purpose and your clarity in relation to why you chose to lead your school.

Stephany Hunter is the headteacher of a rural Suffolk school. As my deputy for seven years, she had regular coaching with me. Like many heads, one of my goals was to prepare my deputy for headship. Steff always had a clear understanding of her own values. Her love of the children and the community shaped her work on our bespoke curriculum. She was driven to serve the pupils through a tailored school experience and galvanised the team around this mission. Steff also brought the core value of patience to her work. She believes everyone has a talent and her patience enabled her to unlock that in our pupils and staff – it was quite remarkable. Above all else, Steff is kind; she doesn't just believe in kindness, she lives it.

I tell you this not just because she has inspired me over the years but because I believe that a values-driven approach helps a school leader build the magic in their school.

In coaching sessions, Steff used the space to work through her challenges and drew on her values to help her. My wish is for every headteacher to have this clarity of their personal values to support them through the fog and make their school a beacon of what is in their own heart.

When the things you do and the way you behave match your values, you feel satisfied and content – happy, even. When we apply this to headship, schools shine bright.

Defining your values

Stephen Covey makes a case for creating a personal mission statement. He argues that by focusing on your personal values, you can reach what you want to be (your character) and do (your contributions and achievements). (Covey, 1989)

Through my work as a coach, I recognise that most people are influenced by a set of values or principles. However, not everyone is conscious of their values. When we define our principles and explore our 'whys', we empower them further to influence our lives and our work.

So how do you clarify your own values? This set of journalling questions, which I use with my coaching clients, will help you with this:

1. Write down a list of things that are important to you and why they matter.
2. Think of a time when you felt fulfilled. What stood out about the way you were living your life or leading your school?
3. What were the most powerful experiences you had as a child? Why did you pick those stories and what impact did those experiences have on you?
4. What will you never compromise on, regardless of anything or anyone?
5. Think forward and write down the legacy you want to leave behind.

Core values are like watchtowers that keep you on the path to fulfilment in your life and prevent you from making painful mistakes. Once one of my clients has clarified their fundamental beliefs through journalling, we then work together to extract the core values reflected in their writing. This is often enlightening and exciting.

Your school is *your* school

While your school's function is to serve the children and families, it is shaped by the beliefs and actions of the head-teacher. One of the aims of Destino Coaching is to empower headteachers to influence education policy. A route to this empowerment is giving you permission to see and own the fact that you are the most significant person in your school. Without the shaping that you do, your school would never fulfil its core purpose, let alone anything extra.

Acknowledging this gives you power that you can then harness to achieve your goals for the community you serve and beyond. This in turns unleashes your authenticity, since you have recognised that 'you being you' is part of the secret sauce that will secure success for your school and the wider community.

Authentic headteachers are the most memorable. They don't play games, nor do they manipulate others. They wear their intentions on their sleeves and make their expectations clear. Authentic leaders are consistent, embrace diversity and encourage their pupils, families and staff to share their ideas.

Your values are your guide rope in the dark

Much of the time, it is complicated, difficult and baffling to achieve the goals you have set for your school. It requires you to think creatively, do things differently and make brain-achingly challenging decisions. When you have clarity on your values, you have something to check yourself against.

At the beginning of the Covid-19 pandemic, I was still in headship. We had no idea what would happen and everyone was scared. Steering the ship was a completely new job that none of us wanted very much. Nonetheless, we found a way through it. My personal strategy was to define some guiding principles, based on my own beliefs. I worked out that the government guidelines made it possible for parents to make decisions in the best interest of their children but did not extend this to school staff. I decided, for the first time in my career, to put the safety of the staff first. This did not mean neglecting our responsibility to the children, but it helped me make decisions about operational matters such as timetabling the in-school provision throughout the pandemic.

This principle was born out of my personal value of fairness, which comes from my childhood. My mother was a socialist and talked to me about the inequalities in society from a young age. This has shaped me more than anything else. I have committed my working life to addressing social injustices through education.

My way was not the only way, but it did come from what I believe and how I behave as a person. As a headteacher, you can never do it everyone's way so giving yourself permission to do it your way is crucial if you are to move forward.

Of course, the landscape changed continually during the pandemic, and I had to reconsider the guiding principles frequently.

Headteachers who lead to leave a legacy are leading for the right reasons. Legacy-building is when the mark you create continues to grow. This is made possible only when you unleash your inner beliefs, which is why a conscious and continual effort to identify your values is so important.

YOUR WHY

In his best-selling book *Start With Why*, Simon Sinek talks about two tradesmen, each spending years laying bricks to build a cathedral which would never be finished in their life-time. One man says he hates his job; he just puts bricks in line every day, every week. The other man is inspired; he does exactly the same job, but he loves it because he knows he is building a cathedral. Whilst the two men do the same job, one aligns with the mission and has a sense of purpose. Sinek makes the point that achievement is *what* you do, but success is *why* you do it. (Sinek, 2011)

In headship, you need your why. You experience increased motivation from making progress, as progress towards your goals is how you find fulfilment, however grand or far off your end goals may be. Having fulfilment means you feel good about who you are and what you are doing with your life. This in turn leads you to a sense of peace because you are clear about what matters. When you have clarity over what matters, you are motivated to contribute more, identify your dreams, and then pursue them. Finding your why pushes you to the place where you find your full potential in the pursuit of your goals.

What made you want to be a headteacher? If you can identify the answer to this, you start to find your why in headship. If you became a headteacher without planning to, what keeps you in headship?

Personally, I took on the challenge because I wanted to address some of the social injustices in our society. The gap in GCSE grades between disadvantaged pupils and their peers is vast and continues to grow. I believe it is fundamentally wrong that the economic circumstances of your parents dictate how well you do at school. This drove me to work in a school that served a disadvantaged community. Our progress in providing working-class children with a good education is what kept me focused on the job.

I urge you to spend time thinking very deeply about this. Why will your work as a school leader matter? What legacy will you leave behind?

YOUR DREAMS

 Let your eyes look directly forward, and your gaze be straight before you."

— *(PROVERBS 4:25)*

Mountain goats can jump nearly twelve feet in a single bound. You may have seen incredible images of goats leaping over canyons. The risk of failure is death but their belief in their ability to succeed is greater than their fear of falling. Even though we are able to achieve our dreams, we often lack the belief in ourselves to achieve them. I want you to identify your dreams and start to call them your goals. Like the goat, your goal is the other side – it's not just a dream.

Imagine you had no fear or doubt. What would you do with your life? Let's say you wanted to run your own business supplying sustainable services to independent shops. Once you identify your ambition, you can dare to imagine it. Not many people take the next step and, say, start to brainstorm business models or research training courses. There is not much of a gap between your dream and making it come true.

To move from one to the other, you have to tame the fear and the doubt.

Now think about your school. What is your biggest dream for your school? Describe your dream version of your school. Dream big for your school and your community. If you start to call this dream your big goal, all you need to do is plot the steps forward.

Let's look at a real example. School X is judged by Ofsted to be inadequate and everything is broken. The headteacher's dream is to provide a world-class education for the pupils, for every child to play a musical instrument, and for the school to support local families to improve their lives through employment and access to good health services. All the headteacher needs to do is start with step one towards the goal. Next, she needs to develop the unwavering belief that it is possible to achieve this goal. At this stage, it is important to look at the evidence and find examples of where similar things have been achieved. This evidence provides her with counterarguments when all the naysayers and doubters join the gremlins in her own head. I have seen countless examples of this at work.

Did you know that Jim Carrey carried around a cheque for ten million dollars for years before he secured the leading role in Dumb and Dumber? He lived believing he would cut a deal that would take him from a poor actor to a successful Hollywood star. His belief in his goal made it possible, as he was able to see obstacles as just that, rather than dream-ending. Once you believe your goal is possible, obstacles simply need managing and removing.

Like the mountain goat, you need to believe, commit, look forward and be unwavering in your pursuit of getting across the canyon.

It is also important you have cheerleaders, particularly if you envisage big challenges along the way. Athletes have a team supporting them, and you need the same, particularly when things get tough and your belief wavers. For me, my greatest cheerleaders were my mentors and my coaches. They ran alongside me at different points in my headship and clapped me from the sidelines at my lowest points.

Now start working towards it, knowing that progress is fulfilling, however far away you are right now from that end goal.

Happy Highlights:

- Strategy must always be underpinned by your values.
- Get your personal values crystal clear. This empowers you to stay on course in life and as a leader. Journalling can help you do this.
- A school is defined by who the headteacher is and what they believe. Owning this enables you to be authentic and to best serve your community.

- Your personal values give you a framework for checking your decision-making process.
- A reason for why you do what you do is crucial to motivate you.
- Dare to dream big: you can leap to a place you never thought was possible for you and for your school.
- Find a mentor or a coach who can help you plan and also cheer you on when times get hard.

2

POWER PLANNING

> *If you service low-impact activities, you're taking away time that you could be spending on higher-impact activities. It's a zero-sum game."*
>
> — CAL NEWPORT, *DEEP WORK*

Once you have clarity on your vision and values, you are ready to plan and strategise so you can achieve your goal. How do you remain focused on the higher-impact activities? This is the question I am asked most commonly as a school leadership coach. The answer is simple, yet challenging: planning, lots of confidence and plenty of discipline.

In this chapter, I will walk you through the planning steps I teach. They will support you to stay focused on your strategy while managing the operational aspects of the school.

When you have a plan, you are being strategic. It means you are shooting beyond your current position in some way, for your school. The same is true if you regularly challenge and question your plan – what are you doing with your time and why? Many headteachers plan their time and even evaluate their use of time but still struggle to stick to the strategic work. Is this you? This is usually because a school is a big pot of distractions and offers a 360-degree view and criticism of you, the headteacher. I want to provide you with an approach that works and the confidence to see your plan through, so you can get the results you want for your community.

Your workspace

I once posted on social media about the importance of your workspace as a headteacher and someone responded with something like, 'I don't have time to be in my office as I am too busy being visible and spending time in classrooms.' Here's the thing: you need to work in a way that enables you to achieve your goals. Promoting one right way of doing things is not helpful, it's distracting. Of course, you will need to be visible and spend time in classrooms, but when you're not, you need to be thinking deeply and completing tasks that move you and your school forward. This is where your work-space becomes important.

Whether you do this work at home, in the coffee shop or in your office at school, I recommend you spend some time getting your environment right for yourself. There are two main reasons for this:

1. To combat procrastination

Most headteachers I have worked with procrastinate on the deep work in some way. This is so easy to do in headship, as there is always a worthy distraction to become involved in. It takes profound self-management to recognise this and to commit to the tasks you may be avoiding in spite of the array of distractions. In my experience, the main reason for this procrastination is a deep-seated belief that you are not capable of achieving your goals. I am here to tell you that you absolutely can. You need to get out of your own way first, and having the right workspace is a trick to help you along the way. I experienced extreme procrastination as a headteacher, alongside hyperactivity. Once I was able to recognise this, I used my nervous energy as a signal to start preparing my office for work. This is how I wrote my SEF, researched curriculum, prepared for governors and so many other tasks associated with strategic goals.

2. To give your deep work status

When you work on an old laptop in a cluttered or busy office, it is like saying, 'This work is not important.' Once you set up a space to do your work, you are showing up for that work and acknowledging to yourself and others that it is of very high importance. By raising the value of the work in this way, you are also more likely to access the creative part of your brain, which you need for working on your big dreams.

Top tips for a good workspace:

1. Make sure you have all the stationery and reference books close by, including a printer (yes, you are allowed to have one for yourself). I like to have highlighters, marker pens, a flip chart, post-it notes, paperclips and a stapler when I'm doing deep work.
2. Check your computer station and chair are well set up so that you don't experience backache or discomfort.
3. Have your workspace cleaned and dusted regularly, especially if you eat and drink in the same space.
4. Keep the space distraction-free when you have time blocked for doing deep work. This means turning off your phone, managing others' expectations of your availability and using earplugs or earphones if necessary. Into the zone!
5. Think about what makes you comfortable. Do you like essential oils, hand cream or other nice smells around you? Maybe certain lighting makes you feel comfortable? I have a water jug and one of my favourite mugs when I sit down to focus on a task.
6. Do you like music in the background? Can you set up a Bluetooth speaker or listen with earphones?

I have worked with a number of executive leaders who have no set workspace and I always recommend they put together a pop-up office. This is a bag, trolley, box or case with everything they need in it to create a workspace that enables you to do your focused work, wherever you are based.

PLANNING STEPS

Step 1 – Set priorities

When you write your strategic development plan, it is essential you identify the three things that, if you achieved them, would move your school to where you want it to be. For two years running, the only key priority we had at my school was to improve academic outcomes for pupils in receipt of free school meals. We knew that if we achieved this, overall outcomes would improve, as would attendance, parent engagement and quality of teaching for all. Most importantly, we would achieve our big goal, which was to ensure all pupils had the same access to opportunities regardless of their start points.

Once you have your key priorities, you must become the expert in these areas. It is essential that headteachers study, research and spend precious time thinking about their key areas of focus. In the example of disadvantaged groups, I read everything I could about disadvantage, the specific challenges of low-income families in coastal towns, where schools were bucking the trend and why. I also invested the small amount of funding we had in high-quality external support for the leadership team in tackling the issues we uncovered. You cannot leave the strategy to chance. Do the deep work before you put a plan together. This is the first essential use of your time.

Step 2 – Plan your month

A monthly plan is significantly more impactful than a termly or half-termly plan. It is a real and immediate timeframe, which increases accountability.

1. Block time towards the end of the month to plan out the following month.
2. Scan ahead and plot out all commitments on a monthly wall planner. Are there things that do not relate to your key priorities which can be moved, delegated or cancelled?
3. Map out all quality assurance work that will take place and check it relates to the key priorities.
4. Block the rest of your time to work on the projects. Define what you will definitely deliver on next month.
5. Update the school calendar with your monthly plan. This holds you accountable and gives a clear message to your team about what you're focusing on.

Step 3 – Plan your week

A weekly plan helps you check you are using your time effectively. It helps you form a mental image of what the week ahead will bring and so increases your chances of success.

1. Reflect on what you have achieved this week and decide what needs to be carried forward.
2. Plot out the week ahead in more detail, with timings for when you will do what.
3. Take into account new things that have come up. Do you need to adjust timeframes?
4. Plot when you will carry out each of the activities on your daily checklist.

Step 4 – Make a daily checklist

Every great leader has a checklist. Atul Gawande was inspired to write *The Checklist Manifesto* after reading a story about a physician who saved a young child who had fallen into a frozen pond. This physician relied heavily on checklists. Many of you will have developed checklists for what great teachers do every lesson, so why not for what you do every day?

I recommend you commit to doing four or five things every day that will influence your school's culture and help you deliver on your mission.

Here is an example daily checklist:

1. Spend time listening to students.
2. Go on gate duty.
3. Recognise the achievement of a colleague.
4. Stop to eat lunch.

You will, no doubt, be inundated with things that hijack your time. Some will even pull on your guilt strings, but please see them as just noise. Nobody will entirely agree with how you choose to use your time as a headteacher, so own it and stick to it regardless. Stop looking for approval. You won't get it until you deliver on your goals, and sometimes not then either!

The secret to being truly strategic in headship is to stick to your plan. In the short term, you might feel strange when you work through a drama or allow other senior staff to respond. However, once you start delivering on your monthly milestones, you'll see that this is what the school needs you to do.

A note on time hijacks

There will always be things that hijack your plan, as schools are dynamic environments. Sometimes you will not have a choice and it will be the right thing to allow the hijack to take over. The key, however, is to make sure it's a conscious choice because then it becomes a strategic decision. Aim for an eighty percent success rate and you will still win.

A note on self-confidence

Leaders need to work on self-belief. We all carry stories with us that nibble away at our confidence. Notice these for what they are and carry on in spite of them. I recommend working with a coach to support you with this. If this is not possible, talk to a trusted mentor, colleague or friend. Discipline is linked to confidence. Back yourself and your plan, and you will stay on track.

As the headteacher, whatever else is going on, you need to prioritise the deep work. Most people around you will not understand this and that is why they are not the headteacher – you are. Give yourself permission to lead your way.

MEETINGS

Peter Hawkins explains that the way we carry out senior team meetings impacts greatly the success of the leaders outside of the meetings (Hawkins, 2011). When I work with senior leadership teams, as a group coach, the first thing I do is observe a series of meetings. This helps me identify questions and lines of enquiry about the performance of the team. This almost always leads us to goal setting for coaching the team.

Most leadership teams spend less than three hours a month on strategy, and nine out of ten fail to execute their strategy. (Forbes, 2020)

These are the most common issues I identify with senior team meetings:

- They spend relatively little time together.
- Agenda-setting is unfocused and undisciplined in meetings.
- Meetings are not decision-oriented.
- Strategy and operations are usually combined into one meeting; operations firefighting always crowds out strategy.

Through my work with senior teams, I have devised a meeting structure that takes into account the need to be strategic and keep on top of the operational matters in schools. This tool can be implemented in more than one way. You may like to consider the principles and how you can apply them to your current meeting structure, to develop a high-functioning team.

I recommend five meetings for your senior team:

1. The daily huddle
2. The weekly senior team meeting
3. The annual strategy meeting
4. A termly strategic refresh
5. A monthly strategy meeting

Operational meetings

1. The daily huddle

This meeting is administrative, covering who's doing what today, where they're stuck, and any opportunities they can share. It saves time by cutting down on email, and clarifying what everyone is doing that day. It is also for sharing what everyone is struggling with and supporting one another with resources to resolve pressing issues.

The process:

Fifteen minutes or less. I recommend you make this a standing meeting, to keep it brief and to keep the energy high.

The huddle is for identifying challenges and helping one another. Further problem-solving might be needed after the huddle between only those people who need to be involved.

If no one raises any issues for more than a few days in a row, you need to probe them a bit more. There are always issues, and this meeting is about finding them while they're still small.

Each person shares:

- Plans for the day
- Things they are stuck on
- Any new decisions or learning

2. Weekly senior team meeting

The weekly meeting lasts sixty to ninety minutes and is scheduled for the same time and day each week. In this meeting, teams drive accountability to the school development plan and identify and resolve issues that get in the way of progress.

Most of this meeting should focus on problem-solving around the obstacles in each key priority area.

The weekly meeting keeps strategic priorities visible, highlights progress towards goals and helps the team to understand any changes that may affect planned activities.

Having this operational meeting means you solve the most important problems fast. You make sure the most important issues get addressed, not ignored.

Celebrating victories together and creating space for personal connections strengthens the team and reinforces cultural values. This meeting can also build trust through guided, constructive confrontation.

Weekly senior team meeting agenda:

1. Review actions list (five minutes)

2. Weekly wins (five minutes)

3. Review key areas:

- Data headlines
- Attendance
- Exclusions
- Joiners/leavers
- Safeguarding referrals (ten mins)

4. Termly priorities and progress (five minutes)

5. Identify top issues (five minutes)

6. Tackle top issues (fifty minutes)

7. Review and confirm actions list (ten minutes)

Tips for the weekly leadership team meeting:

- Agenda items one to five **reconnect the team** with each other, their commitments, and the previously stated goals. This is how you keep accountability to execution.
- Save all discussion about missed targets and execution challenges for items six and seven. Then, **prioritise these problems** before deciding which two or three to tackle.
- Your goal is to **solve a few high-importance issues** each and every week. Don't lose precious time talking about less important problems.
- You have addressed an issue or challenge once the team decides on a course of action and assigns an

owner and due date. To drive follow-up, review this action list at the close of the meeting and at the beginning of the next weekly meeting.

Strategic Meetings:

- The annual meeting establishes the high-level strategy for the coming year.
- The termly meeting reviews progress, adjusts the strategic priorities and sets the specific strategic targets for the coming term.
- The monthly meeting solves a specific strategic challenge.

3. Annual strategic planning meeting

The annual strategic planning process is how teams explore big visions. It is a time to imagine the dream situation of the school in a year's time. You debate and explore these visions so they can be translated into action.

It is best to dedicate at least one or two days to strategic planning every year.

The design of your annual strategic planning meeting will depend on:

- Whether you have an existing plan or are starting from scratch

- The stability of your school
- The size of the senior team

Structure of the annual strategic planning meeting:

1. Vision and mission
2. Personal and school values
3. Priorities
4. Goals and strategies

TERMLY STRATEGIC CHECKPOINT

This meeting requires at least four hours. It also requires that teams face their truths. The meeting will answer the following questions:

- Are the school's actions lined up with the vision?
- How well have the projections matched reality?
- What's going on in the outside world that means your plans need to change?

A term is long enough that teams can see results (or lack thereof). Any longer and it becomes hard for everyone to keep the spirit of the original strategy fresh in their minds.

Consider having the meeting off-site to help the team step away from the day-to-day operations and provide better opportunities for reinforcing the relationships you need in place in order to work through challenging questions.

<u>Aims of the meeting:</u>

- To revisit the plan, review progress towards goals and identify recent events which have impacted the overall strategy.
- To establish clear benchmarks for the next term.
- To strengthen relationships by celebrating wins, sharing key learnings and working together to establish a termly plan to which the whole team can commit.

TERMLY STRATEGIC MEETING AGENDA

1. Welcome and connect

Mention past term highlights.

Highlight key learnings.

Announce goals for the session.

2. Review actions from previous meeting

3. Where we are

Review the school improvement plan.

Review termly progress.

4. Discussion

What went well this term and why?

What didn't go well and why?

What's changed in our overall context in the past term?

What do we need to adjust in our approach next term?

5. Plan the next term

What do we specifically need to start, stop, and continue?

Define new targets.

Define action plan – who, what, when?

6. Confirm agreed plans

Identify key messages to be shared with stakeholders.

7. Close

Anything else that needs to be said?

Tips for the termly strategy meeting:

1. Take a break in the middle. This gives people time to
   talk and think through any hard issues. It also helps
   everyone stay more focused in the meeting and gives
   them a chance to check in on the day-to-day running
   of the school.

2. Keep the discussion structured but not rigid. You are a team working together to drive the school forward – this should feel more like an intense meeting and less like a training session.

3. The meeting can be a good time for the leadership team to evaluate key personnel.

4. Hold the meeting offsite whenever possible. This lifts the status of thinking and planning together as a team.

MONTHLY STRATEGY MEETING

The monthly strategy meeting is dedicated to investigating a specific strategic challenge that has come up. This should be no longer than forty-five minutes.

MONTHLY STRATEGIC MEETING AGENDA

1. Welcome
2. Confirm the challenge
3. Discuss options
4. Decide the way forward
5. Set next steps: who, what, when
6. Set a date to review the outcome
7. Close

Happy Highlights:

- You need a plan if you want to move from dreaming to delivering on your goals.
- Plan your month, using time-blocking for deep work.
- Plan your week so that you respond to the everchanging landscape while staying on track.
- Have a daily checklist that supports you to achieve your mission.
- Make senior team meetings count – separate the operational from the strategic and use meetings as an opportunity to connect and commit.
- Create a workspace that helps you manage procrastination and create the narrative that your focused work matters.

3

HIGH TARIFF RELATIONSHIPS

> *The truth is that stress doesn't come from your boss, your kids, your spouse, traffic jams, health challenges, or other circumstances. It comes from your thoughts about these circumstances."*

— ANDREW J. BERNSTEIN

MANAGING UP

In order to 'win in headship', you first need to acknowledge that you are engaged in a game. A game is an activity involving skill, knowledge, or chance, in which you follow rules and try to win against an opponent or solve a puzzle. While you don't have any distinct opponents in headship, you are surrounded by people and entities that have power over you. To 'win' you need to skilfully navigate relationships in order to deliver on your mission. The puzzle is clear – how do I build a school which provides optimum life chances for the community it serves? It is a highly complex puzzle, especially when you take into account the number of other agendas you have to acknowledge and manage along the way.

You may well work with inspiring leaders who create a safe and exciting environment for you to learn and grow in, and if that is the case, you will achieve your goals as quickly as you want to. It is, however, essential you protect yourself in all relationships where you could ever become vulnerable.

If someone has power over you, you need to consider carefully how you engage in the relationship, as they have the power to make you fall down a snake as well as to help you climb a ladder.

How someone else relates to you, behaves around you or acts towards you is simply information. When our ego responds to the actions of others, we feel flattered, offended, uneasy, shocked, etc. When you interrupt your ego and emotional response, you can focus on what can be learned from the situation instead. In order to protect your sense of self and stay focused on your goals, it helps to consider the three following questions when working with your seniors:

1. What do they want?

2. How can I give it to them?
3. How can I stay on track with my own agenda?

In order to answer these questions, you need to observe (not react) and think deeply.

You may have bravely challenged a senior colleague about their motives, actions and impact on you and your school, yet been disappointed that nothing has changed. In fact, the situation may have got worse. Your challenge may have provoked their motives further. Direct challenge upwards only works when the other party has already recognised they need to change.

A Chair of Governors who keeps finding fault in things you do, for example, might simply be using their platform to make themselves feel personally important as they are emotionally insecure. Ask yourself what they want. Praise? Thanks? Glory? Work out what it is and then find a way of giving it to them. After all, who would begrudge a committed volunteer some praise? They are less likely to go looking for it by identifying faults in your work. You can then refocus your time with them on key priorities and strategic leadership.

It is important you are aware of the role of governors, but calling them out on not complying will be less effective than working with all the unspoken issues that explain their misguided actions.

Case study: imposed consultant

A client came to coaching at her wits' end with an external consultant. This literacy consultant had been assigned to work with her school by her Multi Academy Trust. The headteacher in question had no say in this decision. Week after week the advisor would come in, pick up on something she didn't agree with and 'feedback' to the headteacher. These meetings were stressful, tense, and an unhelpful use of time.

We thought through the situation together and established the following:

1. The advisor had a lot of informal power over the head due to their proximity to the CEO.
2. The advisor wanted to impress the CEO.
3. The advisor was intimidated by my client.
4. The current situation was making my client and her school vulnerable.
5. My client had tried tackling the CEO directly about assigning 'support' and it didn't go well. She concluded that he sometimes used external consultants to fact find for him about his schools and headteachers.

We used this information to formulate these questions:

1. How could my client ensure the advisor said great things about the school to the CEO?

2. *How could she make the advisor more comfortable in the school?*

3. *How could the advisor have an impact on the school?*

4. *What could the school gain from this so that it did not feel like a waste of time?*

My client started to prioritise these meetings in her weekly plan. She built a more positive relationship with the consultant and thanked her for all the support and feedback. She implemented very little change to her literacy curriculum but did come to the meetings with requests for what the school needed, as well as all the things she was proud of relating to her literacy. Within six weeks, the CEO decided to move the consultant to another school.

You have more power to influence up than you think. Influencing your seniors is about accepting the status quo and working with the information you have.

A note on whistleblowing

If your seniors ever do something that falls into the following categories, it is important you seek help from your professional body and follow the whistleblowing policy:

1. A criminal offence, for example, fraud
2. Endangering someone's health or safety
3. Risk or actual damage to the environment
4. A miscarriage of justice

5. Breaking the law, for example, being without the right insurance
6. Covering up wrongdoing

WORKING WITH EXTERNAL PARTNERS

Working with external partners like the literacy consultant above is common in headship. Sometimes you have a say in who comes to work with you and other times, like the literacy consultant, you have to make way for them as part of someone else's agenda. These include consultants, specialists, coaches, charities, health professionals and training providers.

These partners should complement and enhance the work you already do in your school. This is often a brilliant way of introducing, deepening or re-energising an idea.

Here is a list of the main reasons a school engages with external partners:

1. To obtain an external assessment of position or progress in a certain area
2. For recognition and validation
3. For accountability
4. For expertise in an area where there is a knowledge or capacity gap in the school
5. To enhance their professional development package

6. To engage and motivate pupils, staff or parents

To work successfully with external partners, follow these pointers:

Do your research

Speak to several experts before choosing. The cheapest option is not always the best for your school.

Contract the extent of their remit

It is essential that you are clear about why you are embarking on this work with an external partner, as this will enable you to manage the relationship throughout the project. If, for example, you contract a training company to deliver a series of phonics training sessions and they start to give you feedback on the quality of teaching in Early Years, you can put this right easily. However, if your goal at the outset is unclear, you could become distracted by their feedback, when you have your own quality assurance processes in place already.

Their opinion is not your bible

An external expert will usually add direction, knowledge and support to your school, especially if you have worked in partnership with them. Working with the right person, in the right way, can shift a school up a gear. I have experienced this first-hand.

However, working with a consultant is not a substitute for you having your own strategy. You need to own all the initiatives in your school because you know your school best. Be careful to consider the advice of a consultant before you follow it. You, unlike them, have a host of complex matters to consider before implementing something. Not all consultants will understand this and you do not need to explain it to them. Headteachers do not need to explain themselves to external partners (save this for Trust executives and Ofsted).

Be aware of their influence elsewhere

Most external partners have relationships with people who have influence. It is important to be aware of this when forming the terms of your relationship. Ask yourself if your behaviour is worthy of gossip or accolade. A coach should be governed by a professional body and therefore is bound by a confidentiality clause. A maths expert, however, is under no obligation to remain confidential about how they experience you. At best this is a PR opportunity and at worst it can lead to the erosion of your reputation. How you are perceived by others matters, as it is how you gain influence in the relationships around you. So remain formal, friendly, clear and assertive in these relationships at all times.

Enjoy the relationship

As a head, I met some exceptionally talented and warm external partners, some of whom are still friends today. Take your time to find the trust and you may find the strong working relationships here that you can't elsewhere.

SCHOOL GOVERNORS

Most schools have a local governing body and as the head-teacher it is important that you find a positive way of working with them, especially the Chair of Governors. The governance handbook and competency framework (Department of Education) is a great place to start when you are first figuring out the roles and responsibilities of your governors. This information needs to be taken into account alongside the scheme of delegation in your own school, Local Authority or Multi Academy Trust. With this information in hand, you can then devise a strategy for building a relationship with governors that will serve you in your role and will serve the school.

Frustration with governors is a common challenge that head-teachers bring to coaching. This is because governors are often a) non-educationalists and b) don't follow the governance framework. You can ease this by showing that you are the lead professional in the relationship and by being well-versed in the competency framework yourself.

Governors can seem like an unnecessary drain on your time but they actually provide an essential layer of safety for head-teachers and their schools. Governors check you are following your own policies, challenge your decision-making, evaluate risk and provide an invaluable sounding board.

The challenge for you is to build a good relationship with governors while keeping them within their remit and not giving up excessive amounts of your time to their requests.

Without question though, your relationship with your governors is a high tariff one and needs significant care and consideration.

FIND YOUR TRIBE

What is a tribe and why do headteachers need one?

We often talk about 'network-building' in school leadership and there is no doubt that casting your connections net widely helps you to learn and improve. Your network may range from connections with other leaders to expert recruiters or even landscape gardeners – the wider the better in terms of breathing life into your big dreams for your school. Finding your *tribe* is different.

The urban dictionary defines a tribe as, 'a group of people who are loyal to you and care for you like family.' This concept is widespread in the personal development sphere and I talk about it a lot in my work as a coach. My son's long-standing fascination with the Rubik's cube, while exciting for him, was also very isolating. I helped him to find his tribe and he gained more from this than the obvious. His group of cubers shared his joy, related to his frustrations and helped him to be confident about his passions. He says this was the first time he ever felt he belonged somewhere. This experience gave him the confidence to try many new things and find deeper fulfilment.

A tribe is a safe group which means all the members can share vulnerability and build strength as well as develop new and exciting ideas. The feeling of belonging that we get from a tribe helps us establish confidence in who we are and what we stand for. Your tribe shares your values and you feel emboldened by this reflection of what you stand for. This is a higher level of confidence than you can achieve on your own.

It is important for headteachers to get ahead by leaning on each other. You are able to be each others' cheerleaders. The people who are on your wavelength as a leader often stay with you as you move through your career.

Headteachers are quite good at keeping their heads down and getting the work done, but it's important to take the time to look at yourself and think about where your own growth opportunities are. You have reached a level in your career where *you* are your guide. You need to take charge of your own learning and development. It won't be handed to you, so you have to go out proactively and find the things that make you happy and challenge you. A trusted tribe can help you find your blind spots and put things in perspective as well as cheer you on.

I want you to be both happy and challenged in your role and I advocate you finding your tribe to facilitate this.

Where to find your tribe

You need to look for your tribe; it won't come to you. It's all about how you treat opportunities to connect. When you go to a conference, for example, do you challenge yourself to speak to someone new? Chances are, you will align with quite a few people there if you have signed up for the same conference.

There are several ways you can start to link up with a like-minded group. Here are a few to consider:

1. On a course

This is my favourite method as you have a ready-made group with a shared interest that you are scheduled to meet with regularly. I want to challenge you to be the one who links the group up outside the training sessions and keeps the momentum going. I joined a group coaching programme three years ago, and we still meet regularly on Zoom, chat in a Messenger group and have the occasional face-to-face meet-up. Sometimes the connections you make on a course outstrip the value of the course itself and, if you're lucky, you'll get both!

2. Online

You may already be a member of my Facebook group, which I started to help headteachers find their tribe. Since starting the group, I have helped headteachers to create subgroups and find support from one another. There are lots of online communities you can join. I recommend you look out for posts that interest you and respond to others as well as posting about things you're thinking about. You could ask others if they want to create a smaller group to work something through. It could be the beginning of something magical.

3. Through your Local Authority or Multi Academy Trust

You almost certainly belong to a cluster of schools and, while this can be a competitive space, it also has the potential for tribe building. Are there two or three other heads you vibe with at meetings? Could you extend an invite to them for coffee and a catch-up? Take it a step further so you can build a tribe that serves you in your role.

4. Professional events

Do you go to events and conferences and just listen, then head home without speaking to anyone? If so, I want you to make a new rule to not leave an event without talking to somebody. Just say hello to one person. It just takes those small efforts.

Of course, you can belong to several tribes, but the one where you will grow is the one that makes you feel happy and that you belong. Once you find it, never let it go!

You and You

 If you keep doing what you've always done, you'll keep getting what you've always got."

— HENRY FORD

We have all read stories of highly successful individuals who prioritise their personal development. Your relationship with yourself is your supreme relationship and the more you work on it, the better you become at managing the endless demands of headship. A journey within always results in learning, innovation and progress. Checking alignment with your personal values regularly is how you can best achieve this. Do you have a mission in life that you are clear about? How can you refine it?

Here are my top five ways of building a better relationship with yourself:

1. Be compassionate to yourself. Self-compassion can help quieten your inner critic. If your inner critic is noisy, it can help to imagine what you would say to a

friend in a similar situation. Apply those same statements to yourself.

2. Look at the areas in your life that need attention. An important step to improving your relationship with yourself is to reflect on the areas in your life where you are not responding to your own needs, then consider the changes you can make and set boundaries with others around this.

3. Make time for self-care. Self-care is intentionally considering how you can take care of yourself and recharge before you start running on empty.

4. Practise meditation. Meditation can help to change the relationship you have with your thoughts. If you practise it regularly, it can assist in reducing the impact of negative self-talk. Meditation can improve your relationship with yourself and also the relationships you have with others.

5. Keep a journal as a way of shining a light on your values and beliefs about the world and education.

You can improve your relationship with yourself no matter what point you are starting from – progress is not linear. Similarly to any other relationship, you're not immune to criticism, frustration, or feeling disconnected at times. It will take some work and time to build a healthier relationship with yourself, but the benefits of doing so will definitely impact your life and work.

Happy Highlights:

- Come back to your values to guide you in your relationships
- Understand the role of governors and your scheme of delegation.
- Plan meetings with your seniors.
- Think deeply about how to respond to people who have power, formal or informal, over you.
- Find your tribe.
- Remember that your relationship with yourself matters too.

4

THE PUPILS

On dark days in headship, we all need our 'why'. Your work on mission and values will guide you through those dark days. Your ultimate mission is to serve your pupils, and whatever version of service you strive for, your pupils are your ultimate 'why'. For this reason, this book about being a happy headteacher had to include some thoughts on the link between your pupils and your own happiness.

Part of my personal mission statement is: *Believe in something bigger than yourself.* For over twenty years this drove my work as a teacher and a school leader. I now empower headteachers, through coaching, to make system-wide change. Your purpose is like kindling for your soul and, your higher purpose is, without doubt, your pupils.

Seva is a Sanskrit word that means *selfless service*. It is considered the most important part of any spiritual practice in yoga. It lies at the heart of the path of karma yoga — selfless action — and asks us to serve others with no expectation of outcome. You may not be a fan of yoga, but the study of selflessness is something we can all learn from. Many studies have shown that *Seva* is where true well-being is found. It builds strength in our relationships and develops our courage to speak out and advocate on behalf of others when they need us. Yogis believe that the practice of selfless service purifies our hearts and burns away selfish tendencies. There is no doubt that serving others reminds us that there is something beyond our own life goals. Serving your pupils is also about your well-being in headship.

To live a happy life, I have learnt that you need to have some form of service to others. This means teachers have a direct route to happiness and headteachers in particular are very rich in this realm! Contribution beyond yourself helps you maintain perspective and form a strong foundation to build meaning from.

When you just take from the world and choose not to contribute to it (as I said, not a concern for headteachers), it keeps you in survival mode, even if you were to possess all the world's desires!

I find it helpful to go back to Maslow's hierarchy of needs here.

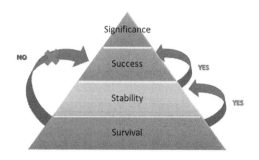

When you contribute beyond yourself at each stage of progression, you both consume and contribute, creating balance. Contribution doesn't just happen at the top of the pyramid, it occurs at every stage. If you focus only on yourself, you won't stay in success or significance and therefore will never reach fulfilment. Success does not always mean personal achievement. Success involves having all aspects of your life working together: job, family, faith, and your place in your community. In other words, your service to your pupils leads to success and fulfilment.

RADICAL ADVOCACY

I encourage you to take service a step further in your role by advocating for the needs of your pupils with guts and determination. I call this radical advocacy and it has four elements:

Supporting teachers to really 'see' their pupils

When schools become bogged down with systems and strategy, a risk arises that teachers start to commit too rigidly to process. This makes things efficient and satisfying but we need to remember that relationships matter more. Your teachers need to see the pupils, care deeply about them and serve their best interests with a good dose of stubbornness. While clear approaches to teaching are essential, so is love. Create an environment where relationships with the pupils come first, and you enable all the adults in the school to understand their 'why'. The pupils need to drive the mission rather than the other way around. In order to do this, it is important that you build space for relationships, talk about pupils as people (not data) and spend time with pupils yourself. Take time regularly to get to know more about individual pupils and imagine their futures with them. Want their success so hard that you get lost in it and this will give staff permission to do the same.

Alicia, a year four pupil, was underachieving and making limited progress in all areas. Her teacher, the SENCo and the deputy head came together to discuss her. The meeting was energetic and they discussed many ideas and interventions. The deputy headteacher drew all the best ideas together and implemented a comprehensive action plan to support Alicia to improve. Everyone was highly committed to making it work.

Six weeks later, Alicia was no further forward and the deputy head was tearing her hair out. The class teacher asked for some protected time with Alicia to understand her better. With just two one-hour sessions with an invested adult, Alicia was able to design her own action plan. She did not make accelerated progress but she started to achieve in some areas. More importantly, she became happier and more able to explain her difficulties. The class teacher stopped seeing her as a barrier to achieving her performance management target and put Alicia at the centre of her planning.

SWEAT THE SMALL STUFF

This is where we do get involved in detail in headship. It is the only place where we must sweat the small stuff.

Playground fallouts and online spats could be considered the bane of a teacher's life. However, try to see the day from the pupils' perspective; to them, this stuff is big. By dismissing pupils' anxieties when they interfere with our plans, we run the risk of teaching them that they don't matter. We all know that self-belief is the most powerful tool for success yet we often risk damaging the self-esteem of our pupils without realising it. This is an example of using your values to drive your approach.

A few years ago, I was watching *The X Factor* and Simon Cowell told a contestant her song choice was wrong as she was too young to have experienced a broken heart. Sharon Osborne exploded and gave what I believe was an inspiring speech about the pain of adolescence. She said his denial of her truth was likely to be more traumatic than the pain she was singing about. We need to bear witness to pupils, especially when their families cannot.

In my school, if a disagreement disrupted learning we regarded it as serious enough to investigate. We made a promise to always offer an opportunity for an upset pupil to be heard. We were not perfect and we did not manage it every single time, but we did most of the time and our children told us they were happy at school.

What seems at first like a small issue, when investigated, can turn out to be systematic bullying. It is only by sweating the small stuff that we work out the big stuff which is at play.

Jazzy's pet rat died and she was inconsolable in school the next day. The teaching assistant working in her class sat beside her and told her she was sorry for her loss. She also helped Jazzy to find the words to express the pain she was feeling, teaching her to use the word 'yearning'. This meant Jazzy felt seen and accepted for something many would laugh about.

Jazzy was in my year ten tutor group some years later and talked about this experience. She said that, for her, it was the biggest pain she had ever felt. She also said the response of the teaching assistant helped her prepare for the loss of her grandmother a couple of years later as she had a language for expressing her feelings. She was able to look back and see there would be greater losses in life than the death of her pet rat but explained that she was very grateful for the space to grieve without judgment for the younger her and the teenage her.

BE NON-JUDGMENTAL

Human beings are hard-wired to make quick judgments so we can decide how we should react to others. This is part of our built-in survival mechanism.

However, this has gradually lost its purpose in day-to-day life and has become a social norm. We judge other people because we do not understand them. We become scared and judge them to 'protect' ourselves. On a basic psychological level, we want to feel safe, so we are at risk of labelling people, including our pupils, as right or wrong, good or bad. This sort of judgment is often learnt from our own childhood experiences. It is essential you protect your pupils from adult judgment in your school.

When children grow up learning to judge the world in a negative way, this can affect their success and happiness throughout their lives. There can be devastating consequences in relation to problem-solving and tolerance for authority, and it sets up the child for a variety of social problems as they mature.

Children enter this world with compassion, and it is crucial we teach them that judgment is unhealthy. We must extend compassion to them at all times, being non-judgmental to them and around them.

Here are my top tips for building non-judgmental behaviours in your school:

Avoid judgmental language

- If we use judgmental language, pupils will too. For example, if we use biased language, children will not only start to use it themselves but will feel judged themselves.
- Try not to make things either right or wrong. Try saying, 'I disagree,' instead of, 'It's wrong.'
- Avoid labelling people as good or bad. In most cases, what we think is bad is just new to us, so we are worried by it. Ask your staff to discuss and debate issues with their pupils so they learn there are many ways to see the same issue.

Use facts, not opinions

People become judgmental when they're unable to distinguish between facts and opinions. Make sure your staff avoid presenting their own views and opinions to pupils. Instead, advocate for discussion based on facts and observations so that pupils have the chance to form their own ideas.

Celebrate diversity

Let your pupils know that everyone is unique and special in their own way through representation and knowledge building. Make sure your curriculum builds pupils' knowledge and awareness of religion, culture, global citizenship, history, LGBT rights and neurodiversity. This not only supports your pupils to grow into rounded, well-adjusted young people but also gives them a clear message that they are loved and accepted by you and therefore by society.

By developing a non-judgmental environment, helping your pupils to grow emotionally and accepting them exactly as they are, you will go a long way towards supporting them to thrive in school and in life.

As a new teacher, I entered the staffroom where a group of teachers and teaching assistants were eating lunch. They were discussing a pupil who was very overweight. I heard them agree he would have more friends if he ate less food and played more football. If staff talk about pupils in this way in your school, children are not safe. This pupil had many struggles and needed our acceptance and support. It is easier to judge than to meet people where they are. School staff can be lazy about how they approach their relationships with pupils because they have the power in the relationship. This child continued to struggle socially and I am sure the judgments of staff compounded his misery. It still brings a lump to my throat as I write this. As headteacher, be sure this is not happening in your school.

FIGHT THEIR CORNER

If you feel 'done to' by the British education system, you can be sure your pupils do too. Just as you can for your teachers, you can filter some of the negative impacts of the system on pupils. This is one of the ways you have the power to influence in spite of the tremendous barriers you often face. Here are my top tips for fighting your pupils' corner:

1. Focus on academic and personal growth over test scores

With high accountability measures weighing on us, it is often easy to fall into the trap of focusing the teachers and pupils on test outcomes. This is rarely motivating. At best it is an endurance test for young people. Even top fee-paying schools invest heavily in confidence-building and extracurricular activities, and in experiences that help pupils learn how to navigate socially.

Being creative unlocks intrinsic motivation in learners. Creativity is found wherever your learners are able to express themselves, flaws and all. So I urge you to make learning in your school about gaining knowledge and personal growth, not about test scores. Great examples I have witnessed of this include:

- Well-planned curriculum content, tailored to the context of the school
- Mentoring programmes
- Sporting and music opportunities for all
- High-quality tutor systems in high schools
- Additional clubs and activities before, during and after school
- Trips, visits and workshops
- A well-run student council

2. No excuses

The media are quick to criminalise young people and label certain socio-economic and ethnic groups. We have an ever-increasing attainment gap between rich and poor children, and mental health issues in the young are rising, particularly among disadvantaged groups. We are bombarded with this news as school leaders and it is difficult not to let it influence our sense of hope for and belief in young people.

As a new school leader in a large inner city primary, I started to focus on the reasons for pupils' underachievement and I risked exacerbating the national excuse culture. I had endless examples of the barriers between some of my pupils and their academic and social success. A brilliant Local Authority advisor bravely called me out and I learnt so much about the risk to pupils of excuses made by school staff. I will always be grateful to her. I began to see the person and potential in every child, which is one of the reasons I became a head-teacher. This is what I want for you and your pupils.

While you undoubtedly need to understand the context of your school in order to plan, it is essential you also arm yourself with all the ways your pupils can fly, so you unlock their potential rather than limit their chances even further. This is true whatever the circumstances of your pupils; we always have the option to look at their circumstances from a deficit or a credit position.

A client shared a story that she used with her staff to illustrate how we are in danger of creating excuses for underachievement. You may have seen or heard a version of the story of a flea in a jar before. It is very fitting in schools and illustrates the risks of an excuses culture...

A flea can jump up to fifteen feet. So, if you placed a flea in a jar, it would have no problem getting out. But if you placed a flea in a jar with a lid on it, the flea would repeatedly hit its head on the lid while trying to escape. After about twenty minutes, the flea would begin to learn that it could not escape and would stop jumping as high as it did to begin with, to stop it from hitting its head on the lid.

Once it became used to the fact that it couldn't escape, even if you removed the lid, the flea would continue to jump the same height, never escaping the jar. Since the flea believes it cannot escape the jar, it stops trying. Because of the experience of hitting its head every time it tried to escape, it would never bother to look up to see that the lid was no longer there.

This sometimes happens in life! We are naturally made to be great, to soar with excellence.

But as life keeps smacking us in the head, we become weary and stop trying to reach our greatness. We impose limitations on what we are able to do and call it 'reality.'

3. Talk about your pupils in every context

In your family, your community and on social media, people will listen to your views. You may not always feel valued by the system, but most people around you will respect your knowledge of young people and want to hear what you have to say simply because you are a headteacher. Use this platform to celebrate the gifts of your pupils and to raise awareness of the issues your face: back them fiercely in public. If every headteacher did this, young people across the country would have a strong voice. Tell their stories, raise their concerns and build support for your pupils as widely as you can.

4. Learn how to navigate to secure what they need

To achieve any sort of useful support for pupils with special education needs or disabilities (SEND), you need to appoint someone on the senior team to become an expert on local systems and structures for securing higher tariff need funding, statutory assessment, brokering of specialist provision placements and access to local health services. There are fewer and fewer resources available so the system for accessing them has become more and more complex. Only those who understand the system are likely to secure support for their most vulnerable pupils. I recommend you nominate a member of your team to volunteer on statutory assessment panels or fair access panels and attend local meetings and conferences about special needs services. This is by far the best way to gain informal knowledge about how best to support your pupils with additional needs.

Find out what local mental health services and charities are available and again, learn how cases are assessed so you can get further faster, for your vulnerable families. My assistant headteacher built very good relationships with social services and this eventually meant we had one social worker allocated to families accessing support services. The same social worker was in our school a day or two per week and we could truly engage in partnership planning for these families.

It is also worth looking into local charities and businesses that support schools and children. I once recruited a governor from Barclays because they offered their employees time off in lieu of governing body meetings. This meant I had an expert in financial planning on our committee, from which our pupils benefitted enormously.

Izzy had complex learning needs. She wasn't like her siblings, which confused her parents. She was well looked after at primary school yet was ill-prepared for secondary school. Her primary school applied for statutory assessment twice, which was refused. Her form tutor in year seven pressed for further assessment. The educational psychology report commissioned by the school concluded that Izzy had Global Developmental Delay (GDD) and the secondary school applied to the Local Authority a third time for statutory assessment. This was again refused on the basis that the school had not demonstrated that they were providing support beyond what was typical for a child on the special educational needs register.

Izzy needed specialist support and the headteacher, the SENDCo and Izzy's parents worked together to appeal the decision rather than accept it. The appeal was upheld and Izzy was eventually placed in a specialist school with an Educational Health Care Plan (EHCP). She learned to read and play the piano and her parents worked with the new school to learn how to support her better. She is now twenty-six and lives in sheltered accommodation. Her school fought her corner and her parents say without that appeal she would still be living at home and unable to read.

WHEN SERVICE TO PUPILS GOES WRONG AND PARENTS COMPLAIN

Why parental complaints hurt

I believe we find parental complaints so hard for two reasons. Firstly, we want to do a good job and parental complaints could be seen as feedback that we are not doing a good enough job (and we love to look for evidence that we are failing). Secondly, they are highly emotive situations that trigger emotions in us about conflict, parenting and other things which lead us to an emotionally vulnerable place. Like many things in headship, you need strategies for resolving the tension. The first step is to intentionally think about how staff and parents interact so that parents feel safe enough to raise concerns informally as often as they want to. This means providing lots of training and support for staff on working with parents.

Even when you have clear systems in place for working with parents, it is likely you will encounter at least a few parental complaints. Here are some common scenarios and suggested strategies for you.

I. When the parent is right

My deputy often said, 'It hurts so much because they are right.' The first thing I say to a headteacher who is agitated by a parental complaint is, to be honest with themselves about what the school may have done wrong. We don't mean to make mistakes, but schools are dynamic, complex beasts and there is always room for human error.

If you or your team are at fault, acknowledge it. Most parents will respond to this openness and honesty with grace and then you can start to work on how you can repair it. Mistakes happen. You need to focus on repair wherever possible, not on defending yourself or your school. Remember, you are not admitting legal culpability by admitting there was not a vegetarian option when you said there would be!

Note, however, that if the error does mean you may have broken the law, you must of course seek advice from your professional body and your seniors before you respond.

When the parent is right, it is likely that a member of your staff has made an error. How you respond to this is an opportunity for culture building. Do you want a school where mistakes lead to growth or one where they build fear, defensiveness and toxicity? Proceed with thought and care.

2. When the parent is wrong

Parents often wade in and complain without the full story. Remember that their child is upset, and they want to protect them so have slipped into fight mode. Remind them you too care about their child and reassure them you will follow up on all their concerns. When you inform them of the facts, be very careful not to appear as if you are gloating or victorious, even if a bit of you is relieved. The parents' error is often an indication that their child has lied or another child or parent has lied and this will need some careful thought and understanding from you. It is also a wonderful opportunity to develop positive relations between the school and the family. Ultimately, working with parents to support the pupil is the best outcome of any situation in which the pupil is unhappy.

3. When the complaint is vexatious

Examples of vexatious parent behaviour:

- Speaking to the member of staff in a derogatory manner and causing offence.
- Swearing, either verbally or in writing, despite being asked to refrain from using such language.
- Using threatening language towards school staff which provokes fear.
- Repeatedly contacting a member of staff regarding a matter which has already been addressed.

Strategies for managing vexatious complaints:

- When the parent tries to reopen an issue that has already been through the school's complaints procedures, inform the parent in writing that the procedure has been exhausted and that the matter is now closed.

- When a decision on the complaint has been made, the parent should be informed that future correspondence will be read and placed on file, but will not be acknowledged unless it contains important new information.

- Limit the parent to one type of contact (telephone, letter, email or meeting).

- Place limits on the number and duration of contacts with staff per week or month.

- Arrange for contact to take place with a named member of staff and inform the parent that if they do not keep to these arrangements, any further correspondence that does not highlight any significantly new matters will be kept on file but will not be acknowledged or responded to.

- Offer a restricted time slot for necessary calls on specified dates and at specified times.

- Ensure any face-to-face contact takes place in the presence of a witness.

In order to serve your pupils, you need a clear strategy to manage parental complaints. This requires you to think about the content and implementation of your complaints policy. Having a plan and an approach helps you focus on the process rather than the emotions it evokes for you and your staff. Managing parental complaints effectively will serve your pupils, and you can do it well, I promise!

Happy Highlights:

- Your pupils are your ultimate 'why'.
- Service to your pupils is a crucial part of your well-being and happiness.
- Sweat the small stuff – care about what matters to your pupils and let your values drive your actions.
- Develop a non-judgmental ethos through language choice, curriculum design and celebration of diversity.
- Fight your pupils' corner.
- Remember that parental complaints are feedback; use them to get better at serving your pupils.
- Write and implement a comprehensive parental complaints policy, including how you deal with vexatious complaints.

5

LEADING TEACHERS

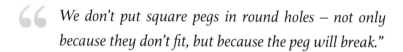 *We don't put square pegs in round holes – not only because they don't fit, but because the peg will break."*

— JANE PROTHERO, HEADTEACHER,
BRADFORD CHRISTIAN SCHOOL

Apart from a short time working as an international head-hunter when I left university, I have only ever worked in schools. I started my career in London as a very keen secondary teacher of Modern Foreign Languages.

New Labour's education policies (1997-2000) saw middle-class and aspirant parents jockeying for positional advantage in education, as well as the inevitable falling prospects for the poor under a government that preached inclusion but pursued exclusionary policies.

Our school served a poor community and teachers who signed up to work there were considered crazy for doing so. We were observed and judged against an abstract set of criteria and nobody seemed to understand what made one teacher good and another a catastrophe. This high judgment and low trust culture meant teachers focused on keeping themselves safe. This took the teachers' energy away from the unquestionable need for us to provide a good education for a community of young people who needed it desperately. My spirit and that of many of my colleagues began to fade and our dreams of enabling improved life chances waned too.

Teachers need to think creatively, experiment and feel safe to make mistakes they can learn from. Blaming teachers for failings in policy first takes the fun out of the job and then kills the potential for brilliance that all teachers have.

When I became a headteacher fifteen years later, I knew that enabling and motivating teachers was the single most important job I had to do. I also knew that I would achieve this in spite of, rather than because of, external structures and policies.

Headteachers often cite dilemmas and anxieties about what teachers in their schools are doing and not doing as one of their top concerns. This fills me with hope for schools. The headteacher who wants to understand their teaching team is a long way down the road to achieving their goals.

With funding at an all-time low in schools, it has never been truer that teachers are our most valuable resource. Supporting teachers to succeed is your top concern. This is how you can navigate this.

Leading teachers well involves three key things:

- Clarity of expectation
- High-quality professional development programmes
- A school culture based on trust and integrity

This is both simple and challenging.

Clarity of expectation

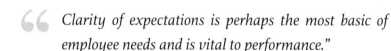 *Clarity of expectations is perhaps the most basic of employee needs and is vital to performance."*

— GALLOP (2015)

There have been 135 changes to education policy in the past fifteen years (Gillard 2018), twelve changes in education secretary and four major changes to the inspection framework. On top of that, many schools and many, many teachers have lived through academisation, re-brokering, amalgamation and closures in that time. It is no wonder teachers are often unclear about what they are supposed to be doing in the classroom. I'm sure you have seen the stats on the number of teachers leaving the profession and all this makes for a challenging landscape when it comes to leading those who choose to remain.

As a coach, I have a commitment to supporting others to find their own solutions. Teachers have been 'done to' for so long, that the culture of the profession has become increasingly toxic and politicised. As a headteacher, you have the ability to remove some of the noise created by all this turmoil, provide a clear framework for teaching and help your teachers be successful while tapping into their creativity.

Teaching is complex – a series of problem-solving activities in quick succession. In order for teachers to become quicker and better at what they do, you need to ensure they have an agreed language of teaching within which to work. For this, I recommend that all schools develop their rubric for teaching, based on well-researched approaches. Liz Robinson, my good friend and CEO of Big Education says that codifying practice enables the sharing of the school's key values or beliefs and provides a foundation to refer back to and hold people to account for. She goes on to explain that, through security building, codification can provide a safety net to fall back on, so it can be a form of contracting.

Essentially codification forms a basis that leads to increased impact, such as the sharing of best practice and innovation, which raises standards and can be made accessible to wider audiences.

Oftentimes, for teachers, it can be difficult to understand the whole process, so codification breaks things down and makes teaching strategies easier to digest. Codification provides teachers with a playbook to guide them, step by step, through various scenarios.

Liz also argues that if your expectations of teachers are too abstract and conceptual, they won't be successful (Robinson, 2023). As I said, teachers need clarity first. This, of course, works best when it is co-created with the whole teaching team. This step comes before developing your teacher development programme, as without it, you lack clarity on what you are supporting teachers to improve.

If you have a document that sets out approaches to teaching in your school, you are almost there. To codify it, you need to dig into the detail of what is meant by each area of teaching so that the whole job of teaching in your school can be learned in small steps. This enables teachers to self-evaluate their teaching and self-identify their next steps, which moves you away from a judgment model to an improvement model. I call this a teaching rubric and I would expect it to be different in each school as well as based on proven and well-researched approaches.

By agreeing on what good teaching looks like in your school, you support teachers at all stages of their careers. Experienced teachers also need clarity of expectation an support with the areas of the codified practice they most struggle with. I always say that expert teachers need to drill the basics and broaden their repertoire. This is how we support them to sustain their expertise and be in a position to model excellence to their junior colleagues.

High-quality professional development programmes

 If our purpose is not to evaluate teachers' performance but instead to help them improve, then the tools of accountability start to look very different."

— *DAVID DIDAU (2020)*

Ask yourself what you want to achieve with your current teacher development approach, then think about how well you actually achieve your goals. If there is a mismatch, I urge you to review and update your approach.

The Education Endowment Fund's (EEF) report on effective professional development identifies three key elements of successful teacher development programmes. The report concludes that schools should:

1. focus on mechanisms, such as revisiting prior learning, goal setting, providing feedback and action planning.
2. build knowledge, motivate staff, develop teaching techniques and embed practice.

3. implement with care, taking into consideration the context and needs of the school.

(Joe Collin and Ellen Smith, 2021)

As a headteacher, I wanted to empower my teachers and I'm sure you do too. However, this requires risk-taking and the courage to be vulnerable, as it means letting go of control. In order to develop teachers, we have to use what we know about how people learn as well as tailor programmes to where teachers are. Teachers don't just improve with experience; they need opportunities to develop new habits and build knowledge.

With a clear framework for teaching, tailored to the school context, leaders can use coaching to develop teaching techniques and provide a safe space for practice, outside the classroom. Instructional coaching is about showing teachers techniques (modelling) and partnering with them to explore how to implement them (practice). This requires you to move away from a model of telling teachers how to teach, leaving them to work it out and then making a judgment about how well they do it.

At Destino Coaching we run a programme called *Coaching in Schools*. We work with leaders to define their language of teaching, or rubric for teaching (codification). We then support the leadership team with coaching models that help teachers find their own way through, with scaffolding, which they know their leaders will protect no matter what is happening outside the school. This requires you to allow for creativity, debate and the emergence of teacher self-evaluation as a starting point for improvement.

'Developing a coaching model with Destino Coaching has definitely enabled our coaches to grow into better leaders. We have all been incredibly appreciative of the new skills that we have learned through coaching. More importantly, though, we have seen improved quality of teaching and the motivation of our teachers to improve, across the Trust, has skyrocketed!'

Jo Cross, Director of Education, Pontefract Academies Trust

As well as instructional coaching, it is essential that teachers have non-directive coaching with someone they trust, to unlock their passion and harness their thinking. With these two strands of professional development, teachers are more likely to be fulfilled, informed and prepared than they are with any amount of after-school information sharing. We now know so much more about cognitive overload but many schools still insist on pouring information into teachers at the end of a full teaching day. You have the power to change this.

I worked with Richmond Hill Academy in Leeds for eighteen months, to support the leaders to implement more effective teacher development approaches. They implemented a menu of professional development that enabled leaders to work with teachers to build their own learning pathways, based on their big dreams for the school and their career goals. All teachers have 'pathway coaching' three times a year; the first meeting is preceded by a self-evaluation against the school's teaching rubric, which they safely and bravely discuss and explore with their coach. All teachers at the school now have access to instructional coaching, leadership coaching and formal study options. Leaders run short, informative sessions for information-sharing relating to curriculum as well as each leading certain aspects of the 'CPD menu', such as their own middle leaders' programme and a leadership book group.

Coaching approaches can be used and developed by anyone – it just takes a brave leader to flip the narrative and start working from the teachers outwards rather than the system inwards.

A note on quality assurance:

It is very easy to confuse teacher development with quality assurance. Many schools check what teachers are doing, tell them what's going well and what's not, and then leave them to improve. While skilful delivery of this message can be developmental for the teacher, it rarely provokes reflection, self-evaluation or deep learning. Sometimes it leads to improvement but this is superficial and motivated by fear of being identified as incompetent. Where teachers become agile and able to make decisions faster, drawing on a wider repertoire of teaching techniques, the professional development structure has created a fear-free space to self-identify where their gaps in teaching may be.

Quality assurance is a process for checking teaching across the school so that you can evaluate the quality of education. I advise my clients to be clear with teachers about why they quality-assure and how the information will be used. Checking is not the important part, so should be regular, quick and undisruptive to learning. Leaders' time is best spent on the thinking and strategy that comes from the data collected. Checking for quality assurance purposes does not need to take up much time for teachers at all. Use their time to discuss their goals and help them practise teaching as well as improve their pedagogical knowledge. Just because we operate in a high-stakes system does not mean that our teachers have to.

School culture

Professor John Hattie's research data reveals that the single biggest factor that affects pupil outcomes is the nature of relationships between teachers and students. According to his research, it has a greater effect than socioeconomic status or reading programmes (Hattie, 2009). Therefore, you need to focus your strategy for leading teachers on enabling positive teacher-student relationships.

Let's think about this for a minute. It's unlikely that any teacher joins the profession without wanting to connect positively with their students, yet I am sure we can all think of many examples of toxic teacher-student dynamics. How does this happen?

We currently operate in a wounded education system. If school leaders do not shape the internal model for their schools, chaos and discord will land on teachers. Stressed, confused and disempowered teachers become disenfranchised. They start to focus on survival rather than the dream and their relationships suffer.

I had a wonderful boss for a short period when I was a headteacher. She told me that my job was to take care of the snakes while my teachers climbed the ladders: she was spot on. We encounter many 'snakes' in school leadership, such as external stresses, parental complaints and inspections, yet they do not need to be big obstacles for your teachers. Your job is to find ways to empower and energise teachers while supporting them to grow and develop. Don't let them get dragged down; wherever you can, slay the snakes for them instead. If you did nothing else in headship, allowing your teachers to thrive would be enough to have a long-lasting effect on your whole community and leave a legacy to be proud of.

Here are some top tips for developing an enabling culture for teachers:

1. Value learning for everyone in the school.

- If everyone in the school is on a path to deepen their knowledge, broaden their experience and develop approaches to work and life, you will be winning.

2. Model positive relationships yourself.

- Be careful not to let your frustrations with colleagues show to other colleagues. This creates an unsafe environment. Instead, make an effort to be curious about your colleagues so this becomes part of the culture of your school.

3. Become a custodian of kindness.

- Call people out when they are unkind: contract what kindness is, and what it is not and hold everybody to it.

4. Protect your teachers from negativity.

- Remember, you deal with the snakes and let them climb the ladders. Just because you are struggling with a new law on asbestos, doesn't mean your teachers need to know about it. Avoid proving your worth by talking about all the pressures and challenges on you from outside the school.

5. Be efficient and organised about the design and implementation of whole school systems.

- Systems and criteria for success make everyone feel safe and this enables them to take charge of their own success.

The quote I opened this chapter with, from Jane Prothero, a participant of my group programme for Headteachers (LEAP™), captures this perfectly. Let teachers find their own way to improve, within a framework they understand, so that they don't break trying to do it in a way that doesn't make sense to them.

We don't need to pamper teachers, but we do need to recognise the complexity of what we're asking them to do every day. Like elite athletes or professional musicians, teachers need support to make small incremental steps towards agility and finesse. It is also imperative that you find ways to involve teachers in the shaping of the systems and approaches in your school.

I cannot move on without a reminder that it is essential to recognise teachers' contributions to the school and the community. I have never met a single person who is not motivated by recognition. Use this wonderful way of connecting with your teachers and with your mission as much as you can!

In order to lead teachers to the best of your ability, you need a few things in place to keep you safe and sane too. Below are my three top tips for bolstering your ability to sustain the effort that is needed to keep your teachers on track:

Contracting

Contracting involves two parties openly and clearly agreeing on how they will work together. At a minimum, these expectations should be discussed; in many cases, you need to write them down so they are available to refer to later.

In my work as a coach, I support leaders to discuss and compose contracts for a variety of reasons, often in response to tension that has arisen. The contracting process with teachers starts with their contract of employment and the official policies you have in place such as the code of conduct, sickness absence policies and appraisal policies. These contracts set out what both parties (you and the teacher) agree to do in the relationship, in certain contexts.

Points to consider when writing staffing policies:

- View them as a contract between you and the teachers.
- Make sure they clearly express what the school needs and offers teachers.
- Involve teachers in shaping them wherever possible.
- Lean into points of potential tension.

- Acknowledge where uncomfortable feelings may surface and plan how you will respond.
- Make sure it is two-way, not just a document that tells teachers 'how it is'.
- Be specific, not generic, so you do not leave room for assumptions.
- Revisit and review these policies annually and date them.

Contracting sets boundaries and increases psychological safety in an organisation. Blurred boundaries with teachers will lead you to culture disruption, a distraction from your goals and situations you may find difficult to get out of.

<u>Space to rant</u>

While it is important that you are the custodian of kindness, it is also important that you have a space to let out your frustrations. This needs to be with someone you trust completely. For me, it was my deputy who listened to me rant without judgment about my frustrations with teachers. If you do not let off steam, it comes out in your relationships. Be careful that this is not always someone in your family so that you keep your boundaries clear between work and your home life.

Honkers

Andy Buck uses geese as a metaphor for leadership. When geese fly in formation, they encourage one another and share the burden of leading so they can travel further (Buck, 2018). In headship, we need people who honk for us, and this includes our school leadership team as well as our mentors and peers. The job is all-encompassing at times and I'm sure you, like many other heads, experience times when you feel like you cannot keep going. This is when you need your team, mentors and peers to 'honk' for you. Be a cheerleader for others and they will do the same for you. This is essential for keeping you going when the task of leading teachers becomes all-consuming.

Happy highlights:

- Create a rubric for teaching, based on proven high-impact approaches.
- Implement a professional development programme that enables teachers to become proficient in this framework for teaching while developing them as people. Coaching models work brilliantly if you are brave enough to rethink CPD.
- Make the job fulfilling and the environment safe enough that teachers have time and space for positive connections with their students.

- Recognise your teachers' hard work and achievements all the time.
- Make sure key staffing policies provide a useful contract between you and teachers and use these policies to guide both parties through tensions and uncomfortable moments.
- Create space to let off steam about your colleagues.
- Build a leadership team that shares the responsibility for leading teachers.
- Keep yourself safe and sane too through contracting, by having trusted people to talk about your frustrations and surrounding yourself with people who cheer you on.

6

HORIZON SCANNING

LITANY AGAINST FEAR

I must not fear.
Fear is the mind-killer.
Fear is the little-death that brings
total obliteration.
I will face my fear.
I will permit it to pass over me and
through me.
And when it has gone past, I will turn
the inner eye to see its path.
Where the fear has gone there will be nothing.
Only I will remain.

— (FRANK HERBERT, DUNE)

This space epic quote is displayed on the wall in my friend Adam's home. Adam came from humble beginnings and, given the opportunity, he pursued a love of music and is now a professional bassoonist. He is a great example of how broadening horizons changes lives. He also knows well that you can only take full advantage of an opportunity if you are prepared to face your fears.

My team and I wrote a curriculum over a period of five years and we called it *Horizons*. We were working in an isolated coastal town and wanted our community to be outward facing wherever possible, in spite of the infrastructural challenges. We were situated in the most easterly point of the UK, so enjoyed the most wonderful sunrises. *Horizons* seemed like a great way to celebrate some of the beauty of the location as well as fill some of the gaps in opportunities we thought our pupils had. When I left the school, one of the parents, who loved photography, gifted me a framed photo of the sunrise seen from the beach near our school. His message read, 'Thank you for broadening the horizons of our boys.' I have the photograph on the wall in my kitchen to this day.

The term 'horizon scanning' is used in a number of sectors and often refers to looking forward and detecting potential disruptions and opportunities in the future. While this is important in school leadership, I use the term here more broadly, to include looking beyond your school; being open-minded and reaching out to other people and organisations for solutions.

Looking outwards is crucial in headship; it is the ultimate *litany against fear*. There is much for you to be afraid of in your role and the temptation is to batten down the hatches, keep yourself and your school safe and do your best, within your school walls. I want you to face your fears, let them pass over you and be brave, so that you can find fulfilment and achieve great things for yourself and your school.

The balcony perspective

What do we mean by 'balcony'?

Heifetz and Linsky (2009) use the expression 'reflect in action by spending time on the balcony and the dance floor' to illustrate how leaders need to metaphorically step away while in the midst of their daily work. This enables you to gain a different perspective and gather insight, not only on issues but also on your own behaviours and beliefs. If you stay over-focused on the operational work without seeing the issues and yourself as part of the big picture, you risk losing sight of the big picture, forgetting what the work actually is (and exhausting yourself with being extremely busy).

The planning tool in Chapter Two was developed in response to the need for headteachers to find ways of being strategic, including standing on the balcony. This is one way of broadening your horizons as it challenges you to think beyond the immediate, scan for issues and make adjustments. This takes courage and requires you in many cases to face your fears.

It is also important to remember that staying 'on the balcony' too long can lead to your team members seeing you as disengaged, or even manipulative.

Knowledge building

Working out what your school needs you to focus on is only a fraction of the mountain you climb as a headteacher. You also need to become an expert in the area of improvement and hold a master plan for bringing it about.

When I work on this with coaching clients, we almost always need to build a reading and research habit. I'm guessing you get drawn in by managing the day-to-day in your busy school and the idea of sitting down to do some reading during daylight hours seems indulgent, unrealistic even. If you take only one thing from reading my book, I'd like you to give this serious consideration. Your school needs you to be learning, growing, developing strategy, and broadening horizons.

In case you do not know these organisations, here is a list of useful sites for researching themes and ideas in education:

EDUCATION ENDOWMENT FUND (EEF)

The EEF is an independent charity that supports schools, colleges and nurseries to improve teaching through better use of evidence. This is a rich source of information and will support the implementation of any new teaching initiative, in any key stage.

https://educationendowmentfoundation.org.uk

CHARTER COLLEGE OF TEACHING

This is a professional body for teachers. They connect teachers and aim to bridge the gap between practice and research in teaching. Dame Alison Peacock is the Chief Executive and her research into what works in teaching is ever present in lots of their resources. They have a fantastic podcast which I highly recommend.

https://chartered.college/

EARLY INTERVENTION FOUNDATION (EIF)

Research on children's physical, cognitive, behavioural, social and emotional development. EIF promotes early intervention and campaigns for high-impact initiatives for the most vulnerable children in our society. Their blog space is particularly useful for looking at alternative strategies for pupils of different profiles.

https://www.eif.org.uk

IES What Works Clearinghouse:

Reviews on research in education with a focus on identifying 'what works in education.' A very valuable resource when you want to check the validity of an idea as they carry out very high level and good quality impact research.

WWC | Find What Works! (ed.gov)

Deans for Impact:

An organisation committed to ensuring new teachers have excellent access to training and continue to learn the best ways to have an impact in the classroom. They have lots of networking opportunities for school leaders who want to challenge old assumptions about teaching and work on the long-term professional development of teachers. They have written some excellent papers on the science of learning.

http://deansforimpact.org

Evidence-Based Education (EBE):

On a mission to improve pupil outcomes, EBE run high-quality, research-based training for teachers and leaders. They also publish regular reports on what works in education.

http://evidencebased.education

For up-to-date research, you can't beat the selection of blog posts, podcasts and reports generated by these groups and charities, but don't forget the value of books. Many educationalists write books and these are often a great source of formal knowledge as well as a support to you as you formulate your own ideas around a theme that you're exploring for your school.

My top tips for building a reading habit:

- Print articles and reports and have a reading file that you work through.
- Read for fifteen minutes every morning or night.
- Use post-it notes for tabs and notes.
- Highlight or underline in pencil.
- Take your current reading everywhere with you and if you end up waiting anywhere for five minutes, read!
- Think of yourself as a student and apply the student techniques that worked for you at university.
- Discuss what you are reading to help you process new concepts and develop mew ideas.

Knowledge building improves your confidence and your ability to take risks, galvanise others and experience job satisfaction. For me, this is the ultimate well-being measure and a sure way to find fulfilment in the role.

Connect with your wider purpose

At the beginning of this book, I asked you to dig deep and consider your personal mission. Can you answer the question, 'Why am I here?' This pursuit of purpose makes horizon scanning, in any of its forms, crucial. We need to think bigger than our own bubbles in order to learn and grow and, in your case, take your school to where you truly wish it could be.

When you think about the kind of world you want to live in, what comes up for you? I ask this because headteachers, collectively, have a shot at shaping the world. Consider how much bigger your work could become if you were brave enough to scan the horizon and shape the future of your school and beyond. Think about the legacy you want to leave through your work, work which I know is all-consuming.

Share what you do

Destino Coaching has a growing blog space for Headteachers to share their own successes and look for examples of projects, initiatives or experiences that will help them in their horizon-scanning pursuits.

I wrote about codifying teaching approaches in Chapter Five. I want to impress upon you the value of this when it comes to sharing good practice too. Spell out how you achieved something for your school. By doing this, you stand up for system-level generosity and a collegiate response to the enormous challenges we face. By creating a macro perspective on something you have done, you create a space where other leaders and teachers can be critical of your work, help improve your work and most importantly learn from your work.

When you look at best practices elsewhere, it can be difficult to understand how they achieved their impact. Big-impact stories are inspiring, but stories that explain how they did it have the power to create a wider impact.

Top tips for writing a blog for other headteachers to read:

1. Make it clear in the title what the blog is about.
2. Give some information about you, your school's profile and what you stand for.
3. State the problem you had.
4. Outline the steps you took to find a solution.
5. Spell out how you implemented the solution.
6. Include a brief impact statement.
7. Include a call to action.

If you have achieved something you are proud of in your school, however tiny it seems to you, I would love to hear from you. I can help you turn it into a blog for our community of headteachers who are looking to learn from you. In exchange, I can find you someone who can show you how they achieved what you are currently working on in your school.

Whatever you share or find, be sure to build your network, as connection with other leaders is the ultimate form of horizon scanning.

Challenge your own view

Looking outwards requires you to challenge your own view and this is where courage and grit come into leadership. Are you prepared to say you don't know the answer or that you thought you knew the answer but you now believe you were wrong?

Through my twenties, I worked with a therapist who told me that she was capable of insights in her seventies that she couldn't have had in her sixties. This was a transformational statement for me. Just by living, working, and being open to evolving ideas, we have new insights. When you actively seek new ways of looking at things, it must follow that you have more insights, more frequently.

You are the headteacher and you are paid to think. Part of that thinking is about finding solutions to things nobody else even sees as a problem. In order to do that successfully you will need to keep challenging your own views. So hold your own hand, tell yourself you'll be there to steady yourself and scan the horizon.

Happy highlights:

- Be brave and face the fears to prevent yourself from becoming insular in your leadership.
- Remember to stand on the balcony regularly.

- Build your knowledge by looking outwards – be a researching headteacher.
- Knowledge building is the ultimate self-care strategy.
- Find your wider purpose and connect with it through your daily work in school.
- When you have something worth sharing, recognise it, codify it and share it with the education community.
- Constantly challenge your own views – human beings have the capacity for new insights all the time.

7

BURNOUT

> *Mental health lies within the consciousness of all human beings, but it is shrouded and held prisoner by our own erroneous thoughts."*

— SYD BANKS

Burnout and boredom can be linked, can be separate, and are often explained by the same issues. I talk about 'crisis fatigue' in headship which, for some, can lead to mental or physical collapse (burnout), while for others it leads to boredom. I will address burnout in this chapter and boredom in Chapter Eight, but you should consider them alongside each other.

IF YOU HIT BURNOUT

We hear a lot about burnout in teaching and school leadership because we are often running on empty. This is a reflection of the strain the school system is under, but it is also a reflection of our failure to adjust to changes in our environment. We are trying to do what we have always done, with a fraction of the resources. This has led us to operate under unrelenting stress both physically and mentally, which does not work long term.

Our well-being is inside of us all and by tuning in to ourselves, we can counter some of the things that lead to burnout, lessening the impact on our lives and our work.

I would bet that you are experiencing some or all of the signs of burnout. Here are the main signs you are heading for a fall:

- Feeling tired or drained most of the time
- Feeling helpless, trapped or defeated
- Feeling alone in the world
- Having a negative outlook
- Self-doubt
- Procrastinating and taking longer to get things done
- Feeling overwhelmed

As a headteacher, I began to normalise these indicators for myself and my senior team. It felt like the only way to keep going. This approach turned on me when my health started to decline rapidly. What started as a small skin complaint became a chronic life-limiting condition – a slipped disc resulted in an eruption and a fractured spine. I self-medicated for anxiety with alcohol. I was forced to take time off work and take a long, hard look at myself. That was a few years ago and I am still working through the impact of the crash on my mind and my body. While I do not recommend leaving yourself to crash, it was a gift for my well-being as it took me on a path that led me to consider my own needs in order to be strong enough to lead and be happy.

Finding your well-being is about being brave and vulnerable with yourself and others. It is about staying with your feelings and responding to your own inbuilt wisdom.

Before my crash, I used to drink coffee when I was tired, skip meals when I was overwhelmed, drink alcohol to stop my brain whirring and buy clothes when I felt bad about myself. While these strategies worked a bit, they took me further away from happiness. I forced myself into mindfulness practice, exercise routines and alcohol-free stints and while these interventions gave me some relief, I had created another layer of things to get stressed about if I didn't do them.

You do not need to strive for well-being, you need to go back to what it is you do that makes you strive for it and fix it.

So I stopped ignoring tiredness, pain, hunger, thirst and anxiety. I stopped myself and started to listen to the basic unmet need. If I was tired, I cancelled a meeting. I slowed down my day instead of drinking more coffee. I made a commitment to eating lunch every day and did not allow myself to go hungry. I started to sit with my feelings in the evening, rather than numbing them with alcohol. All this helped me back to a happier place and kept me in headship longer. I remember walking around the school saying to myself, 'Go gently Nadia, you are weary.'

I have read a lot about personal development. I have a counselling qualification and I am a certified life coach, yet it took a long time before I realised that our well-being is inside of us. I can reduce the impact of my skin condition by not letting it become excessively painful in the first place. The expensive creams and therapeutic treatments are not the routes to well-being for me after all; I just need to interrupt the behaviours that cause my skin to flare up. It is simpler, cheaper and more effective.

What are your barriers to wellness? What do you strive to do to remedy these issues? Maybe you have a bad back and try to fit in an appointment with an osteopath once a month. Imagine if you interrupted the causes of your back pain so that you no longer needed an extra intervention. When you do this, you take out one step and move forward more quickly.

Stop trying to remedy the malfunctions which are caused by ignoring your own built-in ability to prevent them.

When I was looking for a therapist to support my daughter with her relationship with food, I was introduced to Mary, who founded *Light of Mind*. Mary talks about the incredible *light of our own minds* and promises her clients a transformative experience of *discovering their true nature*. My daughter worked with Jess from *Light of Mind* and undoubtedly had a transformative experience. In her words, 'It has helped me see that I have the power within me to fix it; all I have to do is listen to my body and care for myself. It is not easy but it is quite simple.'

When we view well-being as trying to atone for the sin of falling apart, not only do we create more pressure for ourselves, but we also create shame, which leads us further away from happiness.

You may think that headship does not allow you to slow down and listen to yourself, but the truth is that you are the only one who has a choice about how you do things. So I urge you to consider what you currently do for your well-being and ask yourself if it takes you back to yourself, where your built-in system has the answers.

While my hope for you is that you will stop and think before you find yourself in the state I got into, it is likely that some of you are very close to crisis and unable to carry on. In this case, you need a roadmap back to somewhere safe. Below is an outline of the five steps I go through with my coaching clients who are in this position.

1. Do not resign!

The autonomic nervous system has two components: the sympathetic nervous system and the parasympathetic nervous system. The sympathetic nervous system functions like the accelerator pedal in a car. It triggers the fight-or-flight response, providing the body with a burst of energy so it can respond to perceived dangers. Your body actually thinks your life is under threat and so resignation seems sensible. However, your life is unlikely to be in immediate danger and making a big decision based on false information may not serve you when you reach emotional safety. You may well decide to resign further down the road to recovery but now isn't the right time, even though it feels like it is.

2. Secure your safety

You cannot make decisions or manage effectively when you are in an emotional crisis. I recommend the following steps to secure your emotional safety as quickly as possible:

- **Prioritise your basic care needs.** Drink water, eat food, go to the toilet and sleep for a minimum of eight hours each night.

- **Grieve.** Make space to acknowledge things have not turned out as you planned. Allow yourself time to be sad or cry until you can reach some level of acceptance from which to take the next step.
- **Surround yourself with people who make you feel supported and safe.** Make time to see and speak with the people who make you feel seen, heard and supported.
- **Create space.** Taking some time off work, even one week, will make a significant difference to how you feel. You need space away from the trigger in order to process its impact. Cancel plans and delay errands and engagements outside of work too. This reduces distraction and noise at the time you most need space for your emotions to stabilise.

3. Get help

When friends and family ask what they can do, allocate them chores or childcare support – reduce all the demands on you as much as you possibly can. Buy in support if you can afford it. This is important for three reasons:

- It gives a signal to the body that you are out of danger, as there is no pressure on you or your time. Then you can think more clearly.
- It makes more of the space you have created so that you can stabilise more quickly.

- It helps you accept that you are in crisis and that pushing on is not an option.

4. Focus on yourself

Make the time and space you've created *count*. Focus on you unapologetically for set times each day and, if possible, large chunks of time. You may find it helpful to work with a professional counsellor or coach to get the maximum benefit from this.

5. Connect with your well-being

Listen to your body and respond to its needs. Will a gentle walk feel nourishing? Are you thirsty or tired? Check in with yourself frequently and identify your care needs.

If you follow these steps, you should feel more grounded within a week or two but sometimes it might take longer. This does not mean you're 'fixed'. It means you can start to manage some tasks, put a recovery plan in place and consider what your next steps might be with more clarity.

After a crash, it is a long road to recovery. While you will grow and learn from the experience, you can avoid it altogether by stepping in now and taking your mental and physical health seriously. Preventing burnout is part of your success criteria, as you can only achieve your goals if you are there to do so. Headteachers work in a high-pressure environment and will burn out if their only strategy is to work at their capacity limit for sustained periods while ignoring their well-being needs.

Happy highlights:

- Think about which signs of burnout you are already experiencing.
- It is important to find your own well-being by getting to the cause of the burnout symptoms, rather than load more pressures on with well-being 'treatments'.
- Tap into your inner wisdom to find your happy place.
- Follow the five-step plan to cope with crisis and do not act from a place of panic.

8

BOREDOM

 We are not given a short life but we make it short, and we are not ill-supplied but wasteful of it."

— *SENECA*

IF YOU GET BORED

D o you find it difficult to stay focused for more than short periods? Or do you find yourself lacking interest in school life? These could be signs you are bored. You may have started to notice an absence of excitement or a general decrease in your motivation to do the job. These are the most common ways headteachers describe boredom to me. If this is you, do not worry, there is much to be gained and a number of ways forward. If it isn't you, you may find it useful to read on so you are aware of the signs and associated struggles to look out for.

I think it's fair to say that I became bored of headship periodically. I have reflected on this a lot since becoming a coach and I believe, looking back, that each time I became bored, there was a gift in it for my school. Each boredom phase saw me make changes or improvements that helped the school move forward. The last one was a move away from the school, when staying would not have been the right thing to do anymore as I had a new calling. Like all other emotions, boredom needs attention if we are to grow and learn as people and leaders.

The ancient Roman philosopher, Seneca, wrote about the restlessness of boredom and its importance in directing us to fulfilment. In his book, *On the Shortness of Life*, he reminds us about the non-renewability of our most important resource: our time. The quote that opens this chapter comes from this book and is worth our reflection. Seneca believed that feeling bored was a sign we are detached from the things we can control, which leads us to focus more on our inner lives. This, he argued, is an opportunity for growth.

Being and Time is a philosophical text written by the twentieth-century German philosopher, Heidegger. In it, Heidegger explores the meaning of being and of human existence. Heidegger thought the concept had been misunderstood and he wanted to ground our understanding in the everyday experiences of people, a novel idea at the time. He was interested in the notion of 'authenticity' and made the case that boredom can lead us directly there. If we consider that boredom can drive us to an uncomfortable place where we might look inwards at ourselves, this makes sense.

If you find yourself unmotivated, lethargic even, in your work, ask yourself, 'What is going on for me?' and, 'What will it take to pique my interest again?' The common experience of boredom can help us to get to what we truly want next. This varies for each of us but bored headteachers most commonly tell me they want more of the following to help them find their mojo again:

Autonomy

Connection

Recognition

Creativity

New learning

Let's take new learning as an example. You have more or less learned the role and you want to learn something new. This opens up a range of possibilities. Explore as many as possible through journalling or with a coach or mentor to reveal something that lights you up. For one of my clients, it was studying for a master's degree; for another, it was moving to a special school from a primary school, within the same Trust.

In both cases, boredom gave them the opportunity to reflect and listen to what was lacking for them. I call this 'leading from your truth' and I believe it is the only way to lead well. There is much to take from Heidegger's work but the power of leaning into your boredom is incredibly relevant to head-teachers. It highlights that we really need to listen to ourselves, which will ultimately lead us to a happier, more authentic place.

When a client talks to me about feelings of boredom, it excites me. Reflecting on boredom in headship often leads to insights about what needs to change for the headteacher and for the school. It is a challenge point that can result in powerful personal and professional development.

Let's delve into the main causes of boredom in headship, then outline the possible ways forward for headteachers who are starting to find the job dull. However much gift there is in boredom leading to personal growth, we cannot ignore that lack of motivation and action in headship can be disastrous for schools.

When I became bored in headship, I had an overwhelming lack of interest in things that had previously fired me up. I remember sitting in my office wishing something dramatic would happen to engage me!

What causes boredom in headship?

Boredom can be caused by a number of factors but the three main causes I have come across in headship are being stuck in monotony, loss of autonomy or crisis fatigue.

Repetition or monotony

It takes a few years to develop expert knowledge in leading schools because many things you have to tackle only come around once a year. Take exam season, for example: you only manage access arrangements once and don't do it again for a whole twelve months. But once you've done it a few times, you know all the pitfalls. Then you can move quickly and confidently through the process.

Once you have mastered the basics of leading a school, you are able to predict possible outcomes in most situations due to your secure knowledge in most domains. This makes you very accomplished in headship as you can make better decisions, more quickly. It can also be a very comfortable place to be as your confidence is high. Many headteachers enjoy this phase, relax into the role and become even more effective than they were early on in their headship. Others (like me) miss the adrenaline of making decisions in new contexts where there is a constant element of risk-taking.

Heads who find peace in this place sometimes only enjoy it for a limited period and so, like heads who don't like this mode at all, they can also get bored later down the line.

Absence or loss of autonomy

Autonomy is your ability to make decisions for yourself. Other people can either undermine or enhance your autonomy but you never lose the ability to be autonomous.

Autonomy gives you choices so that you do things of your own volition, and the choices you make are the source of your own actions. The way your managers and leaders frame information and situations either promotes the likelihood that you will have autonomy or undermines it.

It can be demoralising when you feel divorced from the strategic decision-making in your school. Many of my clients discover this to be the cause of their boredom. When you sign up to lead a school, you want to shape the journey and reach the destination you chose for your school. When this is withheld or taken away from you, your motivation in your work inevitably suffers.

If you have a manager or leader who holds the reins on you very tightly, this could lead to boredom if you are unable to negotiate your autonomous space within the relationship.

If absence or loss of autonomy is the cause of your boredom, your only ways forward are to work on your relationship with your seniors by deepening connection and trust and managing upwards or by moving on. Moving on is one of the options I will expand on in this chapter. For tips on managing upwards, you can pop back to Chapter Three.

Crisis fatigue

Not all headships are the same but all headships are challenging. When the challenge is relentless crisis management, some headteachers lose interest in the project due to the feeling of never moving forward with their dreams. Being stuck in fire-fighting mode can become demotivating as you start to feel like your presence and endless hard work makes limited or no difference. This can lead to a form of burnout that is experienced as boredom.

Ways forward when you are bored in your headship

1. Reshape your headship

Expert headteachers who have become bored can reshape their headship. There are many ways to do this and I have supported many coaching clients to negotiate changes to their role. These include:

- Executive headship (taking on a second or multiple schools)
- Taking on a whole cluster or trust responsibility
- Working as a consultant a few days a month
- Swapping responsibilities with your deputy
- Taking on more teaching responsibility
- Supporting another school
- Studying or embarking on training that will help you reshape the direction of your career and your school

- Study something that interests you

In order to identify a change that will best suit you and reshape your headship, you first need to identify what is missing. On a few occasions as a headteacher, I had a yearning to have a wider impact on the community so I looked for opportunities within our local cluster of schools to support projects within the area. This had the effect of reshaping my headship as it changed how I made decisions and engaged with other schools and how I saw my role within the community.

Expert headteachers who have become bored would do well to look at where they can increase the challenge. By challenge, I do not mean stress! I mean doing things in the role that are new to you and mean you are learning and growing.

2. Take a break

When I took part in the Talented Leaders Programme (TLP), we had a talk from an ex-headteacher who had taken a career break between headships. She got bored after a few years in headship, retrained as a homeopath and opened a practice in North London which flourished for several years. Then one day, a friend sent her an advert for the headship in the school she had attended as a child. She applied and was successful. She explained to us that the break made her better, faster, and more focused for a whole host of reasons.

I had a client who inherited a large sum of money and resigned because she was bored of headship, without knowing what she'd do. She spent a year renovating her house and working on her health and well-being then returned to headship in a very different school, which suited her newly discovered priorities outside of work. Two years on she continues to be a head and her school brings her great joy and fulfilment.

Taking a career break can seem daunting at first, but it could be one of the best decisions you ever make. Career-wise, a break could help you reconnect with who you are and find motivation again. That's not to mention the personal benefits to your overall well-being and sense of self-worth.

Another option is taking a sabbatical. Sabbatical leave is an extended time away from work that is granted to an employee for varying purposes, including personal reasons, for professional and academic growth, or for learning and development, while maintaining their status as an existing employee. This is becoming more common in headship as many Trusts recognise the benefit of holding open a post for a strong leader who needs some time out.

If you do resign and take a break, you might worry about finding a headship after a break. I have met countless heads who have done this and successfully secured a new role when they were ready, so you can too. It is worth considering how you present the benefits of your break in your new application, including all you have learned and how ready you are for the challenge of headship again. Like with all headship interviews though, it is important that the school and Trust or Local Authority are a good match for you.

3. Move on

Headteachers who are suffering due to a loss or lack of autonomy in the role have two options: manage up or move on. Moving on can be a very sad and challenging decision and finding the next role can take some time. However, a new headship, with the right Trust or LA for you will be better than staying where you are with a diminishing level of motivation.

4. Do something else

Occasionally I work with a headteacher who has become bored and decided to leave the profession. I was one of these headteachers and my reason for leaving headship to become a coach was a desire to give headteachers across the UK a voice. I couldn't do that in headship or by working with one Trust or LA. This decision increased the challenge level, refreshed my purpose and motivation and also enabled me to continue supporting the profession. I have no regrets. I have learnt that we have many transferable skills following head-ship and I believe a headteacher could switch careers and be successful in almost any other sector. If you are considering leaving the profession, I urge you to do your research and spend some time delving into what else lights you up. Well-being comes from fulfilment and if we have to work, our work needs to matter if we are to find happiness.

Boredom and ADHD (Attention Deficit Hyperactivity Disorder)

I have worked with quite a few headteachers who have ADHD. I think the job suits neurodiverse people, so this does not surprise me. I could not, therefore, write about boredom without pointing out a few things about ADHD and boredom.

If you have ADHD, your brain consistently seeks stimulation and you likely crave mental and physical tasks that hold your interest. When you get bored, you might suddenly zone out on the task at hand, fidget, or seek interest elsewhere. This is completely okay and my wish for you is that you are able to recognise what is happening and allow yourself to do what it takes to hold your interest or to flit and look for something else to work on. It is likely you are good at starting things off so make sure you have set it up for someone to finish and move on. Remember, your pace and creativity are gifts to the school and to society.

People with ADHD have less diffusion of dopamine in the brain's synapses than neurotypical people, so they do not get the same degree of satisfaction from doing ordinary tasks. That lack of satisfaction is felt as boredom, and it can decrease your motivation to continue. If this is you, it is essential that you plan a challenging or creative task every day, when mapping out your week. It is also essential that you prioritise rest outside of work, whatever that looks like for you.

Happy highlights:

- Boredom can be an opportunity for growth.
- Boredom is not great for your school.
- Boredom is caused by repetition and monotony or lack of autonomy.
- Tackle boredom by reshaping your role, moving to another school, taking a break or doing something else.

9

BE ASSERTIVE

 Never retreat. Never explain. Get it done and let them howl."

— *BENJAMIN JOWETT*

Assertiveness is the skill that will best help you to manage yourself, your people and headship. Being assertive helps you influence others as it helps you gain acceptance, agreement and behaviour change. Once you give yourself permission to make your priorities the priority, people begin to organise themselves around them and you achieve your goals more quickly while earning respect from others.

Being assertive is the ability to express your opinions positively and with confidence. Simple, yes, but very challenging for most of us!

What I want for you in headship is that you feel in control of yourself and that you are honest with yourself and others. Without this, you cannot do the deep work that brings about lasting change, which is why I have included this chapter.

In some ways, it is easier to explain what assertiveness is not than what it is. As leaders we think big, make a plan, and then get to work. Then, with frequency and unpredictability, we come across obstacles. If we do not do the work on how to manage those obstacles so that we stay on track, we are likely to become either passive leaders or aggressive leaders. Sometimes we are both!

AGGRESSIVE RESPONSES

Do you ever lose your temper or snap impatiently at people at work? This is aggressive and, while understandable in headship most of the time, it is not your fastest route to getting back on track. While people readily accept aggressiveness from their leaders, they don't like it. It reduces the influence you have over people's intrinsic motivation. You need to be considered in headship if you want to achieve your big dreams for your school. This requires you to seek approval from yourself and contain your emotions when you are frustrated. A client recently told me she wanted to rip someone's head off and when she told me why, I wanted to help her do it! We agreed that this would be unhelpful.

The thing is, anger is about how a situation affects us emotionally, and showing you are angry creates two problems. Firstly it makes you vulnerable, as your staff see the shape of your heart and unless you have complete trust with everyone in your school, you allow yourself to be open to manipulation. Secondly, anger takes you down a rabbit hole when you need to be running along the track at a good pace. Stop and look at the rabbit hole and remind yourself you don't need to go down there – even if it's very tempting, it is a distraction from your goal. People who achieve focus relentlessly on their goals.

PASSIVE RESPONSES

Many headteachers allow themselves to be drawn into the obstacles, let themselves be taken off their path and risk losing their way. Have you ever been drawn into a timetabling issue when you should be doing your planned work? Or do you drop everything for a particular member of staff who has learned very well how to manage up? Sometimes the passive response is simply allowing the problems that come up to be the excuse for not delivering on your goals.

As well as being passengers of the demands on you from your staff, you are also at risk of responding passively to your own seniors (Chair of Governors, CEO, Regional Director, etc). Fear of how you may be regarded by those senior to you can prevent you from challenging them so you comply even when their plans do not suit you or your school.

A leader who asks you to prepare a set of data the afternoon before you finish for a half-term break is being aggressive. The work needs to be done but, by giving you no warning or reasonable timeframe to complete it in, they disregard your needs and feelings.

A passive response would be to cancel the family plans you have the next day and get it done over the weekend, dreaming all the time of finding a new job in which your holidays are actually holidays.

When, on the other hand, you inform the leader that the work will be done but only after you return from the break, you hit the sweet spot between passivity (not being assertive enough) and aggression (being hostile, angry or rude). You assert your rights while recognising your boss's need to get the job done.

I have never known this to go wrong for a client but it does require you to be at peace with the fact your line manager or Chair of Governors might be secretly annoyed with you for managing them so well!

Both aggressive and passive responses make sense when the challenges are overwhelming, as they so often are in headship. In fact, as human beings, we see any form of conflict as a threat and we will always have these default responses. We can tell our brains there is no threat and respond in ways that will help us achieve what we want more quickly and with greater impact. I want you to have some strategies for overriding these responses and responding assertively to tension.

Being passive is defeatist, aggression is setting out to win, but assertiveness is based on balance (and we could all do with a bit of that).

It is also worth considering how your actions could elicit passive or aggressive responses from your own staff. If you notice those responses, it may be that you are making unreasonable demands on your own team members.

Of course, you may be a headteacher who has few or no demands made of them by your Chair of Governors. This can be challenging for other reasons and can also lead to passive and aggressive behaviours in you. Look out for it!

THE BENEFITS OF BEING ASSERTIVE

Assertive people make great leaders!

Being assertive rather than aggressive with your colleagues leads to a culture where people feel comfortable voicing their opinions and working through problems with others, building strong working relationships. Assertive leadership fosters teamwork instead of competition.

This motivation to work together towards goals is made possible because your team feels valued and has more motivation to tackle the challenges that school life throws at them. When school culture strengthens this community environment, people experience greater job satisfaction, meaning they are more likely to stay. The longer your team stays together, the better the school will become.

Being assertive helps you to negotiate successful "win-win" solutions. People see you as a problem-solver and feel safe around you as you show your belief in finding solutions, rather than in causing stress and fear.

The greatest benefit of being assertive is how it builds your confidence. You dare to protect your needs in your professional relationships while maintaining respect for others. This means you stay on track and reinforce the message to yourself that you and your plans matter.

Risk warning:

- Some organisational cultures prefer people to be passive and may view assertive behaviour as a threat.
- Research has suggested that gender can have a bearing on how assertive behaviour is perceived, with

men more likely than women to be rewarded for being assertive (Maxfield 2015).

- There is also a risk that you could go too far. If you become too assertive, you may stop listening to others despite them having good ideas. This could alienate your colleagues and damage relationships.

- Remember the importance of knowing when you have been triggered emotionally and practise not responding immediately. Develop some ways of buying yourself time and space so that you can respond in a way that helps you achieve what you want to in the situation.

HOW TO BE ASSERTIVE

1. Value yourself

Go back to your true beliefs and values. Do you always have to put others' needs before your own? Do you believe that makes for a fair world? Are there times when it is important that your needs are met too? Does being aggressive align with your core beliefs about how we should relate to one another? How would you advise someone else about asserting their needs and are you following that advice? Listen to yourself and be bold enough to act on what you truly value.

If you have been taught to be 'nice', it is likely that your default response to tensions is to be passive, as you don't think it is right to put your needs first.

Dr Aziz Gazipura, in his book, *Not Nice*, argues that *'Being nice does not come out of goodness or high morals. It comes out of a fear of displeasing others and receiving their disapproval. It's driven by fear, not virtue.'* (Gazipura, 2017)

With this in mind, ask yourself if being passive is actually kind. Kindness is about holding the desires and needs of others in your heart as you make decisions. This becomes more and more challenging as you compromise your own needs for theirs. Resenting someone is neither kind nor helpful.

If on the other hand, you are someone who becomes aggressive when the needs of others get in your way, it is likely that the desire to defend your position and prove your worth takes over. It comes back to the need to value yourself in order to be able to respond appropriately to frustrations.

Neither approach leads you to a strong position. The first step to developing assertive approaches to obstacles is to work on the way you value yourself.

How you go about this depends on who you are and what your story is, but it starts with telling yourself you are worthy. With coaching clients, I often support them to notice their thoughts and to interrupt them and decide what the new ones will be. Until you do value yourself, you will struggle to be assertive.

2. Voice your needs and wants confidently

I have worked with many headteachers on how to voice their needs confidently. Here are my top tips:

- Slow down your speech. Most of us speak quickly when we're nervous. Before explaining your needs in a situation, be mindful of slowing down your speech.
- When there is a pause in the conversation, let it be. Rushing to fill a silence creates unnecessary noise and can dilute the message. Appearing comfortable with silence is very powerful.
- Try not to have conversations to the side either with other people or about another topic. We often do this in headship as we try to solve lots of issues at the same time. When voicing your needs, this is not a helpful habit as it is another way you might dilute the message.
- Lower your tone. If you speak in a high pitch or vary your vocal range, try lowering it or smoothing out the variations (practise this on your own). This helps convey a calm and confident message.
- Work on your posture. As a headteacher, I practised yoga and Alexander Technique. When I improved my posture I felt an improvement in my communication. I have helped many others to do the same.

3. Acknowledge that you can't control other people's behaviour

All you have is your response to others and that is the key to being assertive. Make peace with the fact you cannot control others and work on how you respond in different situations. Even the strongest, most talented people cannot control what others do. Clinical Psychologist Carla Marie Manly explains that the need to always be in control is a destructive fear that can take hold of your inner world. Whereas constructive fear alerts us to an actual threat (such as an intruder or unfriendly dog) and keeps us safe as we navigate life, destructive fears do nothing but erode our overall well-being. Trying to control the behaviours of others is exhausting; it also prevents us from developing tools to respond to situations. When we practise this skill we reduce our fear and we successfully navigate more and more situations.

4. Express yourself in a positive way

Positive framing makes people less likely to feel like you are attacking them. Instead of, *'I am sick of your last-minute demands on me'*, try, *'It is so much easier for me to manage my time when you give me a few days' warning.'* Language and phrasing are crucial to successful assertiveness. I suggest the following techniques for expressing yourself positively when asserting your position:

- Use 'I' statements.

- Show empathy with their position.
- Ask for more time if you lose confidence in your position.

5. Be open to criticism

The main reason headteachers tell me they feel they cannot say no to people at work is fear of being criticised. We want to be liked. We want people to consider us leaders who do the 'right thing'. However, this is not always possible so I want you to work on being open to criticism. By making peace with the fact that others will take issue with your decisions, you can be free to follow your plan and confident to say no when it is necessary. You are in charge so believe in your ability to make the decisions that best serve you and your school in each moment.

6. Learn to say "no"

Saying no is a trade-off between being helpful and being in control of your work life. It can increase your credibility with your staff. When we lose control, it no longer matters how helpful we are as we are not working on the things that will make the most difference. Therefore if you are not comfortable with saying no, you need to learn how.

We associate saying yes with being a team player, showing we can handle it and be successful. If the word *no* is hard to say, you can say it by giving a *qualified* yes. Say yes but only to a time and approach that suits you. Don't drop what you're doing every time someone asks something of you. Then follow through with what you have agreed. That makes it a yes, but on your terms and without losing control of your own work.

There are usually two things you need to practise saying no to:

- When a member of staff asks you for help or advice, you could offer an alternative time or suggest another person who could help. 'Could you finish the planning tomorrow? I have some space after lunch to go through it with you.'
- When your manager or leader asks you to do extra work, you could negotiate by offering to do it but point out what you are already working on based on the plan you previously agreed. 'I will happily do this but I may need to push out one of the other tasks.'

Your objective when saying no is to free up time to make it manageable, even if you do end up doing it eventually. Your tone when delivering your 'no' is very important. Your aim is to make your colleague feel valued without overcommitting yourself or compromising your own priorities.

Some emergencies will require you to drop everything and this is expected of you in school, but make sure you are using your judgment rather than acting from a place of fear about how others will view your course of action. Nobody in the school holds as much information as you, nor does anyone else understand all the pressures you are under. They never will, so you cannot expect them to understand your rationale for every decision you make.

7. Review your progress

Make time regularly to reflect on how many times you have said 'no'. Consider how this helped you to maintain control of your work, your relationships and how it made you feel. If saying no is very challenging for you, I recommend working with a coach to develop a confident mindset around being assertive and self-appreciation.

Happy Highlights:

- Assertiveness is about prioritising your needs while recognising the position of others.
- Aggression never works.
- Passive responses slow you down and can alienate you from your work.
- There are risks to assertiveness in a psychologically unsafe environment.
- Assertiveness is a skill that takes practice.
- Start practising assertiveness through conscious language choice.

10

FINAL WORDS

I set out in this book to help you work on the most common things that cause headteachers to feel defeated. I have drawn on my experience as a headteacher and coach, and I hope you have found it succinct, digestible, relatable and useful.

Above all else, I hope you take away a renewed commitment to your well-being. Finding your well-being gives you your best chance to avoid burnout or boredom, or indeed, to recover from them if you have hit a wall. While navigating relationships, try not to lose sight of who you are and what you stand for. In other words, avoid spending precious time and energy on trying to become the version of yourself you think you should be or the headteacher you think others are looking for. The deeper we look in the direction of our truth, the more likely we are to see it and to find happiness in our work.

We all make errors and we all experience triumph; it is human and you are only human. Remember to see your faults as evidence that you belong with others, doing your best to navigate headship and learn. Learning to fully accept yourself is your route to your well-being. I hope this book has helped you feel brave enough to explore that path. This starts with giving yourself permission to look at the challenges differently, separate them from who you are as a person and tackle them your way, knowing that you are valued, whatever the outcome.

It is imperative to have a set of values to guide you in your work as a headteacher. In my work as a headteacher coach, three core values drive me:

1. Empowerment

This is the heart of my mission. With profound self-belief and understanding of your worth, you can reach your full potential and achieve the best possible outcomes for your school. Therefore, whenever I design a programme or work with a headteacher, I focus on empowerment.

2. Challenge

I challenge people. That is my approach to relationships, including the one I have with myself. This is one of the values that makes me who I am, and I bring this to coaching. I am excited by human potential, and I know we cannot achieve our big dreams without safe and true challenge.

3. Love

This value makes some people feel uncomfortable. However, I could not escape it when I started to define my driving values. When we feel deep affection for others, we are motivated by their progress, success and reparation. That is how I connect with my clients and I make no apology for it.

What are *your* core values? How do they drive the way you live and lead? Reflect regularly on this and check that your values define your actions, wherever possible.

I am sure you have a mission statement for your school and that you revisit and review it frequently. Think about your *personal* mission statement as well. What matters to you? Think about every aspect of your life. Write your personal mission statement and display it for daily inspiration. It keeps you in check.

Here's mine as an example:

Spend time with those you love
Embrace challenge
Put your passions centre stage
Care for your body
Make time for silence

Visit beautiful places
Believe in something bigger than yourself

Headship is first and foremost about service. Your service to your pupils, your staff and your wider community is what makes the job so crucial – it is also why we feel the high stakes so acutely. When you ask a child what they most value in a teacher, they say, more often than not, a teacher who cares. Make this a priority in your school, however challenging that is in terms of building a culture that enables rather than blocks safety for children.

Your teachers are your greatest asset in the service to your community. My hope is that you will always make teacher development a priority in your school, whatever else is happening. Investment in teachers is an investment in the future and you hold that in your hands.

When I moved to Lowestoft from London I filled teaching posts with people from all over the UK and abroad. This was an effective strategy for a couple of years and then they all went home. I realised that the long-term recruitment challenges of working in a coastal town needed a more sustainable approach. I sat on the beach with my deputy one May with three teaching posts to fill for September and we came to the conclusion we had to recruit locally by offering more than other schools offered. Our way through would be excellent professional development opportunities. In the next few years, we supported four unqualified teachers through achieving Qualified Teaching Status (QTS) as well as sustaining a razor-sharp focus on teacher development. It wasn't perfect but it was the best we could do with the resources we had and we never again sat on the beach in May with three vacancies for September.

The underpinning philosophy that carried us through the next stage of our journey was 'listen not tell'. I had to become a better person in order to do this. I enrolled in a counselling course and saved to fund my coaching certification. I trained in the States over a summer and within a few months I was coaching my senior team and many of my teachers.

Coaching teachers makes sense to me. I set up Destino Coaching with the aim of supporting other Headteachers to find their own way through the madness that is headship. I have become a better person by learning to listen and support. Every day I am inspired by the strength of people's love and commitment in the profession.

Asserting your needs is not just about self-care. It is also about achieving what you believe to be right for your school. That is why I have included it in this book. Practise expressing your needs while acknowledging those of others. Reduce, avoid, then eradicate aggressive and passive responses for your own self-esteem and to enable you to best serve your staff and pupils.

If you have read this far, I hope that means my book has helped you in some way and I thank you for all you do in your work – it matters. My dream is that all headteachers have a voice that enables united system-wide change: this starts with you and your self-belief. If you are interested in working with Destino Coaching, I have set out below the ways we currently support headteachers.

WHAT'S NEXT?

1. Join my free online community

I have a closed Facebook group for headteachers where I offer daily support, encourage healthy debate and connect headteachers from around the world. You are very welcome to join us and contribute.

https://www.facebook.com/groups/5144922005628650/

I hope to see you in there soon!

2. Work with a coach

We now have a team of certified coaches at Destino who are all either serving or former headteachers. We offer 1:1 coaching for headteachers at any stage of their journey. I coach up to fifteen headteachers at any one time and I also offer one pro-bono slot each year. I challenge all my clients to stretch their capacity by asking for far more than they have done before.

At Destino Coaching, we use a non-judgmental approach while being open and honest about what we hear and see. Coaching is confidential, developmental and safe and we pledge to provoke you into action. We offer warmth and sincerity and take pride in making sure our clients feel their goal has been achieved through coaching. We keep in touch with clients between sessions and continually improve our coaching skills through our own ongoing professional development.

Types of coaching we offer:

Leadership Coaching

Leadership coaching identifies leadership strengths and areas of improvement for an individual or a team. It focuses on developing emotional intelligence and defining a future vision for oneself as a leader.

Executive Coaching

Executive coaching is for leaders and improves leadership abilities as well as the challenges associated with managing organisational change.

Life Coaching

Life coaching supports the client to create a more fulfilled life. We identify values, purpose, goals and dreams while recognising barriers. We help people take action towards goal achievement.

We use a combination of these approaches as most head-teachers need all three!

3. Join my group programme for Headteachers: LEAP™

LEAP™ runs twice a year and in the programme I teach tried and tested ways of tackling some of the tough bits of head-ship. Using the power of the group, I facilitate group coaching as well as reflection on different aspects of the role. This is very popular and I continue to improve and refine the content. Courses start in September and January.

4. Coaching in Schools Programme

This is an instructional coaching programme for schools. When you sign up, we work together to explore how coaching approaches can support your mission. We focus on profes-sional development models for teachers, making coaching work, codifying teaching approaches to make them coachable and leadership coaching. This is a year-long comprehensive programme. Destino provides training, support and coaching to introduce and implement your unique coaching programme alongside your leadership team. This can include coaching for pupils, staff, leaders and parents.

I would love to hear from you!

Nadia

nadia@destinocoachinguk.com

DESTINO.COACHING_NADIA

https://www.instagram.com/destino.coaching_nadia

https://twitter.com/DestinoNadia

https://www.facebook.com/NadiaDestino

ACKNOWLEDGEMENTS

Without my Mum, I would not have written this book. In the last year of her life, we talked about our shared hopes for education and she encouraged me to write more so that I could reach more headteachers with the message that their voices matter. She did not live to see the book in print but her influence is ever-present in all I do. Thank you for loving me so fiercely, Mum.

I have some very special headteachers to thank:

- Stephany Hunter for partnering with me as my deputy when I was a headteacher: without you I would not be where I am today. I am so proud of what we achieved and what you have gone on to do.
- Anna Mackenzie, the best friend I could ever have wished for and the most extraordinary headteacher: you make me feel like I belong.
- Liz Robinson for your unwavering love, friendship and inspiration throughout my career.

Thank you also to my fabulous beta readers, Katherine Finch and Jane Prothero, who helped shape this book into something they believed headteachers needed.

Lastly, without the patience, support and belief of my husband, I would never have found the courage to start Destino, let alone write a book: you are my world, Mike.

BIBLIOGRAPHY

Buck, Andy, <u>Leadership Matters 3.0: How Leaders At All Levels Can Create Great Schools</u>, John Catt Educational Ltd, 2018

Covey, Stephen, <u>The Seven Habits of Highly Effective People</u>, 1989

Sinek, Simon, <u>Start with Why</u>, 2009

Cal Newport, <u>Deep Work</u>, 2016

Hawkins, Peter, <u>Leadership Team Coaching</u>, 2011

Gillard, Derek, <u>Education in England: a history</u>, 2018

Hattie, John, <u>Visible Learning</u>, Routledge 2009

Joe Collin and Ellen Smith, <u>Effective Professional Development -Three recommendations for designing and selecting effective professional development,</u> (EEF), 2022

Liz Robinson, <u>Big Leadership Adventure – Codifying Guide</u>, Big Education, 2022

Gallup, <u>State of the American Manager Report</u>, 2015

Sheryl Sandberg, <u>Lean In - Women, Work, and the Will to Lead,</u> 2013

Andy Buck, <u>Leadership Matters</u>, 2018

Seneca, <u>On the Shortness of Life</u>, Penguin Books, 2005

Heidegger, <u>Being and Time</u>, Harper and Row, 1962

Heifetz R A, Grashow A and Linsky M (2009). <u>The Practice of Adaptive Leadership: Tools and Tactics for Changing Your Organization and the World</u>, Cambridge, MA: Harvard Business Press.

Ames, D. & Flynn, F. (2007). <u>What Breaks a Leader: The Curvilinear Relation Between Assertiveness and Leadership</u>, Journal of Personality and Social Psychology, 92 (2), 307–324.

Gazipura, A, <u>Not Nice: Stop People Pleasing, Staying Silent, & Feeling Guilty... And Start Speaking Up, Saying No, Asking Boldly, and Unapologetically Being Yourself</u>, B.C. Allen Publishing and Tonic Books, 2017

Lee, S. & Crockett, M. (1994). <u>Effect of Assertiveness Training on Levels of Stress and Assertiveness Experienced by Nurses in Taiwan, Republic of China</u>, Issues in Mental Health Nursing, 15 (4), 419–432.

Marie Manly, C, Joy from Fear: Create the Life of Your Dreams by Making Fear Your Friend, Paperback – 1 April 2019

Maxfield, D., Grenny, J., & McMillan, C. (2015). Gender Inequality: Women Judged More Harshly Than Men When Speaking Up Assertively [online].

Pourjali, F., & Zarnaghash, M. (2010). Relationships between assertiveness and the power of saying no with mental health among undergraduate students, Procedia - Social and Behavioral Sciences, 9, 137-141.

Printed in Great Britain
by Amazon

27045244R00090